Embracing Crowns for Governmental Intercession

Transforming the Earth
Through the Authority
of Crowned Intercession

By

Dr. Ron M. Horner

Embracing Crowns for Governmental Intercession

Transforming the Earth
Through the Authority
of Crowned Intercession

By

Dr. Ron M. Horner

LifeSpring Publishing
PO Box 5847
Pinehurst, North Carolina 28374 USA
www.RonHorner.com

Embracing Crowns for Governmental Intercession

Transforming the Earth Through the Authority of Crowned Intercession

Copyright © 2025 Dr. Ron M. Horner

Scripture is taken from the New King James Version®. Copyright © 1982 by Thomas Nelson. Used with permission. All rights reserved. (Unless otherwise noted.)

Scripture quotations are taken from the Amplified® Bible (AMP), Copyright © 1954, 1958, 1962, 1964, 1965, 1987 by The Lockman Foundation.

Scripture quotations marked (NLT) are taken from the Holy Bible, New Living Translation, copyright ©1996, 2004, 2015 by Tyndale House Foundation. Used by permission of Tyndale House Publishers, Carol Stream, Illinois 60188. All rights reserved.

Scripture marked (THE MIRROR) is taken from The Mirror Study Bible by Francois du Toit. Copyright © 2021 All Rights Reserved. Used by permission of The Author.

Scripture marked (KJV) are taken from the King James Version of the Bible. Public Domain.

All rights reserved. This book is protected by the copyright laws of the United States of America. This book may not be copied or reprinted for commercial gain or profit. The use of short quotations or occasional page copying for personal, or group study is permitted and encouraged. Permission will be granted upon request.

Trademarks are the property of their respective owners.

Requests for bulk sales discounts, editorial permissions, or other information should be addressed to:

LifeSpring Publishing
PO Box 5847
Pinehurst, NC 28374 USA

Additional copies available at: www.ronhorner.com

ISBN 13 TP: 978-1-953684-71-4
ISBN 13 eBook: 978-1-953684-72-1

Cover Design by Darian Horner Design
(www.darianhorner.com)
Image: 123rf.com #85093814

First Edition: July 2025

10 9 8 7 6 5 4 3 2 1 0

Printed in the United States of America

Table of Contents

Acknowledgments i
Foreword iii
Characters Mentioned ix
Preface xi
Chapter 1 Your Crown of Authority 1
Chapter 2 The Crown of Governmental Intercession . 19
Chapter 3 Factors In Governmental Intercession 27
Chapter 4 Directive to the Sons 69
Chapter 5 Retrieving Lost Crowns 77
Chapter 6 Strategies of Hell Against Crowns 83
Chapter 7 Basic Categories of Wickedness 87
Chapter 8 The False Crown of Deception 91
Chapter 9 The False Crown of Loathing 111
Chapter 10 The False Crown of Fear 127
Chapter 11 The False Crown of Magic 143

Chapter 12 The False Crown of Secrets 159

Chapter 13 The False Crown of Antichrist 175

Chapter 14 The False Crown of Devouring 191

Chapter 15 Gaining Freedom
from the Seven False Crowns 207

Chapter 16 Superior Crowns 213

Chapter 17 Heavenly Assistance 217

Chapter 18 Fruit Inspectors 223

Chapter 19 Strategies for Engaging
with Angels and Principalities 229

Chapter 20 Epilogue 233

Appendix 235

Learning to Live Spirit First 237

Petitions for Divorce 245

Petitions for Divorce from
the Sun God & the Moon God 247

Petition of Divorce from the Sun God 249

Petition of Divorce from the Moon God 277

Resources from LifeSpring 307

Description 313

About the Author 315

Other Books by Dr. Ron M. Horner 317

Acknowledgments

Almost daily, Stephanie (my COO), and I have engaged Heaven concerning the crown's revelation. We knew it was vital and timely for the Body of Christ. As the sons move further into their sonship, the revelation of the crowns will be even more critical.

I wish to thank Stephanie for always being willing to engage Heaven for revelation. I honor the gift within her and bless her.

I bless my lovely wife, Adina, for her contributions and ongoing support, and my youngest daughter Darian who has worked so diligently to see the Crowns Series of books produced.

Thank you.

Foreword

In the tapestry of human existence, few symbols carry the weight and wonder of a crown. It evokes images of royalty, authority, and triumph—yet its truest meaning often eludes us, buried beneath layers of earthly pomp. Dr. Ron Horner's study on crowns invites us to peel back those layers, revealing a profound spiritual reality that transcends time and culture. With a voice both tender and bold, Horner beckons readers to explore the crowns bestowed upon us, not by human hands but by the divine.

In every society, governmental leaders wield extraordinary influence. Presidents, kings, legislators, and governors shape the course of nations, determining policies that affect millions of lives. Their decisions ripple through economies, cultures, and histories, making their roles both powerful and precarious. Yet, the Bible reveals that their authority does not exist solely in the physical realm. Beyond the visible struggles of politics and governance lies a spiritual dimension where forces of good and evil vie for control.

This unseen conflict, known as spiritual warfare, targets governmental leaders with particular intensity due to their capacity to sway entire populations. At the same time, Scripture offers a counterweight to this battle—promises of divine wisdom, protection, and blessing for leaders who seek God's guidance.

In Ephesians 6:12, the Apostle Paul writes, "For our struggle is not against flesh and blood, but against the rulers, against the authorities, against the powers of this dark world and against the spiritual forces of evil in the heavenly realms." This passage clarifies that the actual adversaries are not human beings but spiritual entities operating behind the scenes. Governmental leaders, as stewards of earthly authority, become focal points in this cosmic struggle. Their decisions can either advance God's purposes or serve the agenda of darker powers, making them prime targets for influence or attack. The Bible illustrates this dynamic repeatedly, showing how leaders rise or fall based on their response to these unseen forces.

Consider King Saul, Israel's first king. In 1 Samuel 16:14, after his disobedience leads to the departure of God's Spirit, "an evil spirit from the Lord tormented him." Saul's subsequent descent into jealousy and paranoia reflects a leader overtaken by spiritual oppression. His erratic behavior—hurling spears at David and consulting a medium—demonstrates how vulnerability to spiritual forces can destabilize governance. Similarly, in Daniel 10:13, a "prince of the

Persian kingdom" delays an angelic messenger, hinting at spiritual powers assigned to influence nations and their rulers.

The attacks on governmental leaders today take various forms, each designed to exploit their position. One prominent avenue is the temptation of pride and power. Proverbs 16:18 warns, "Pride goes before destruction, a haughty spirit before a fall," a truth vividly illustrated by Nebuchadnezzar in the book of Daniel. The Babylonian king, basking in his achievements, declares, "Is not this the great Babylon I have built... by my mighty power?" God humbles him, reducing him to a beast-like state until he acknowledges divine sovereignty. Today, leaders might face similar lures—public adulation, unchecked authority, or the thrill of control—pushing them toward self-reliance rather than dependence on God. When pride takes root, it blinds them to wisdom, opening the door to ruinous decisions.

Deception is another weapon in this spiritual arsenal. In 1 Kings 22, King Ahab seeks counsel before battle, only to be misled by lying spirits speaking through his prophets. Despite Micaiah's warning, Ahab follows the false voices and meets his demise. This narrative echoes in modern governance when manipulative advisors, biased media, or half-truths that obscure reality sway leaders. The Apostle Paul notes in 2 Corinthians 4:4 that "the god of this age has blinded the minds of unbelievers," a blinding that can extend to leaders who reject divine insight. Whether through flattery or misinformation, deception distorts their ability to govern justly.

Opposition and persecution also mark this warfare, particularly for leaders striving to uphold righteousness. Daniel, a high-ranking official in Babylon, faced a conspiracy from jealous peers who tricked King Darius into condemning him to the lions' den (Daniel 6). His faithfulness to God provoked their hostility, yet divine intervention preserved his life. Contemporary leaders who champion biblical values—opposing corruption or defending the vulnerable—may encounter similar resistance from political rivals, cultural elites, or public backlash. The pressure to conform can be relentless, testing their resolve.

Moral compromise rounds out these assaults. Pontius Pilate's encounter with Jesus in John 19:12-16 exemplifies this struggle. Knowing Jesus was innocent, Pilate nonetheless yields to the crowd's demands, swayed by threats to his political standing. Leaders today face similar dilemmas: approving unethical policies to appease constituents, bending to corporate interests, or silencing their conscience for expediency. Satan, described in John 10:10 as the thief who "comes only to steal and kill and destroy," exploits these weaknesses to maximize disruption. One compromise can unravel a leader's integrity, amplifying harm across their sphere of influence.

Despite these threats, Scripture equips believers—and leaders—to resist. James 4:7 offers a clear strategy: "Submit yourselves, then, to God. Resist the devil, and he will flee from you." Submission to God erects a spiritual shield while active resistance repels the enemy. For leaders, this might mean prayerful decision-making, as Paul urges in 1 Timothy 2:1-2: "I urge, then, first of all, that petitions, prayers, intercession and thanksgiving be made for all people—for kings and all those in authority, that we may live peaceful and quiet lives in all godliness and holiness." Prayer becomes a weapon, dismantling strongholds and aligning leaders with divine will.

Blessing and prosperity flow to nations under godly rule. Psalm 33:12 proclaims, "Blessed is the nation whose God is the Lord." King Hezekiah's reign illustrates this. By restoring worship and purging idolatry (2 Chronicles 30-31), he ushers in a season of abundance for Judah. Leaders prioritizing God's principles can expect similar favor—perhaps not always material wealth but stability, unity, and moral flourishing. This promise hinges on their faithfulness, as Proverbs 29:2 contrasts: "When the righteous thrive, the people rejoice; when the wicked rule, the people groan."

Divine guidance further empowers leaders. Psalm 32:8 pledges, "I will instruct you and teach you how you should go; I will counsel you with my loving eye on you." Despite his failures, David sought God's direction.

He earns the title "a man after God's own heart" (1 Samuel 13:14). Leaders who consult God—whether drafting laws or negotiating peace—receive tailored counsel, aligning their governance with eternal purposes.

Dr. Horner has crafted not just a book but a journey that beckons every reader to look beyond the temporal and claim the eternal. Crowns are a gift, a mirror, and a map, guiding us toward the throne where our true selves are crowned in everlasting light. Taste and See the Lord is good.

The Honorable
Dr. Neal Jackson
North Carolina State
Representative
District 78

———— ∞ ————

Characters Mentioned

Adina – Dr. Ron Horner's beautiful wife, co-founder, and Chief Financial Officer of LifeSpring

Einstein – the physicist of 20th Century fame.

Malcolm – a man in white who tutors us in the things of Heaven.

Mary Magdalene – the woman who washed Jesus' feet with her hair.

Stephanie – serves as the Chief Operating Officer of LifeSpring International Ministries, Inc.

Lady Wisdom – the entity that carries and imparts wisdom. See Proverbs 8.

———— ∞ ————

Preface

This year is a critical year for the sons of God. Whether you are on the blue side or the red side, America and the world are at pivotal points. Paul instructed us to pray for kings and all that are in authority. He also said, in Romans, that the powers that are in place are put in position by his hand. That is an understanding that many wrestle with. In Jeremiah, the prophet was instructed to pray for the peace of the land that Lord had brought him into for when the land was at peace, he would prosper *and* be at peace. I am sure all of us want that to be the situation. I heard Heaven say this as I journaled recently:

> *The understanding of the Crown of Authority is huge for My sons. They have not known of this directly, but that will change. Understanding that everyone has a Crown of Authority, but some have allowed it to be polluted with mixture from the elements of the world and from feasting from the wrong tree. I will unlock solutions for dealing with the mixture in people's crowns so*

they can live out of the authorization given by Me for their crowns.

This book will unpack for you how to apply the understanding of crowns to governmental intercession. As sons, especially sons who know about the Courts of Heaven prayer paradigm, it is incumbent upon us to properly utilize those understandings and apply them to our efforts of intercession for our nation and the nations of the earth.

Some who will read this book are specifically anointed to pray for the President or the primary leader of your nation. Others are called at this season to pray for the senior tiers of leadership in your country, regardless of the form of government. As an American, I will address issues directly related to our situation, but will also try to broaden the discussion to include broader intercessory contexts.

We have been given an extraordinary revelation regarding the subject of crowns that we are just beginning to understand. As the revelation is unpacked, not just by me, but by others in the Body of Christ, I believe freedom will come, and we will be able to position ourselves for a move of the Glory of God throughout the nations of the earth.

We can pray for revival all we want, but we need to address the legalities that are hindering the move of God in our nations.

Isaiah 49:24-25:

> [24] *Shall the prey be taken from the mighty, or the* **lawful captive** *delivered?*
>
> [25] *But thus saith the LORD, Even the captives of the mighty shall be taken away, and the prey of the terrible shall be delivered: for I will contend with him that contendeth with thee, and I will save thy children. (KJV)*

The Lord, in this passage, asks Isaiah if you can free someone who is a lawful captive, and the answer is no, not without dealing with the legality that positioned the person to be taken captive. How many of our leaders are lawful captives?

A basic premise of the Courts of Heaven prayer paradigm is:

> *If you have prayed repeatedly for something, and the answer has yet to come, there may be a legal reason why. If we deal with the legal reason, get it resolved in the Courts of Heaven, and the answer will come.*

The primary solution to the blockage is repentance and forgiveness. We are told in Matthew 6 that we can't be forgiven if we don't forgive. Repentance is the solvent that removes the glue causing hindrances to our prayers. The Father is willing to answer our prayers, but we must cooperate with him. Much of our intercession in times past has involved asking God to do something and simply ignoring the things that may have been hindering us, instead of addressing the legalities and having the blood of Jesus applied to those situations, so answers could readily come.

When you hear me say "pray" for something, I typically mean using the Courts of Heaven paradigm as the basis. It is a type of prayer, but it is usually fashioned differently than the other types of prayer with which we are familiar. When I say we "prayed" for someone, that often means we accessed the Courts of Heaven on their behalf and received righteous verdicts from the courts.

Often, our governmental leaders are living under the influence of a barrage of accusations, false verdicts, or ungodly bonds. Many are operating under the influence of ungodly assignments of witchcraft or similar things. Some are first workers of darkness, then politicians. Some have supernatural, ungodly hedges that provide a semblance of protection, allowing wicked agendas to gain traction and be implemented. Part of your governmental intercession will involve the destruction of these hedges by the angels of Heaven and the construction of godly hedges around our political leaders to protect them and their families from harm.

Fortunately, we have learned effective means of dealing with these things through the Courts of Heaven. This book will encompass the recent revelation of the Crowns of Authority and other crowns we carry or need to carry. As we implement these concepts, I believe we will see breakthroughs on multiple levels, benefiting our state and nation.

Often, you will see someone who is elected to office who seems very promising on the surface. They seem very sincere, but in six months, you can barely recognize the person you voted for just a short time ago.

What happened? The office or the seat of that office was contaminated, and the newbie stepped into a place that had not been cleansed of the prior contamination and was eventually consumed by it.

This contamination factor shows up in several of the false crowns. We must repent for those who created the original contamination and those who perpetuated it throughout the years. Ask for a cleansing of the office from all spiritual debris and all evidence and dedications of that office or seat to any demonic entity. Using the Petitions for Divorce in the Appendix might be advisable.

In the United States, the government system has three main branches. The Executive Branch comprises the President, Vice President, and Cabinet. The Legislative Branch consists of the various representatives of the citizens, whether Senators, Congressmen, or Congresswomen. The third branch is the judicial branch of government, which consists primarily of the United States Supreme Court.

Each of these arenas requires prayer and court work to be done on its behalf. However, you may only be assigned to a particular area within the government.

We must fulfill our roles and remain in our assigned positions.

In addition to praying for these officials, you are praying for them to walk in integrity, wisdom, righteousness, and sonship. You pray for their protection from wrong people, situations, and influences. It only takes a few moments to abolish someone's career.

In this book, we will explore how to remove false crowns and replace them with the Superior, godly Crowns of the realms of Heaven. The Superior Crowns will replace the inferior, ungodly crowns and the false crowns discussed later in this book.

How the Father sees us is usually not how we see ourselves. How the Father views our nation's political leaders often differs from how we perceive them. Exposure of things, situations, and people often needs to occur to root out the wickedness in our nation.

1 Corinthians 4:5:

*Therefore judge nothing before the time, until the Lord comes, who **will both bring to light the hidden things of darkness and reveal the counsels of the hearts**. Then each one's praise will come from God. (Emphasis mine)*

According to Proverbs 14:34:

Righteousness exalts a nation, but sin is a reproach to any people.

We will repent for the unrighteous deeds of our national and state leaders. The Father desires good for you, your family, community, state, and nation. He does not want evil for us.

We MUST remember that "what you honor you have the benefit of. What you dishonor will exit your life." We must honor the men and women who are leaders of our nation. It is a huge responsibility, and they can do their job more effectively if they are honored rather than despised.

You may be a staunch Democrat, but that does not mean you cannot honor the man or woman in office. The Office of the President deserves respect, for Romans says the powers in place are put there by God's design. To disrespect them is to disrespect the choice that God made, and you are ultimately disrespecting God.

President Donald J. Trump is the formal title of the current president. He is not "Trump, the Donald, or any other familiar or disrespectful name. For Americans, he is your duly elected President and deserves respect.

In the book of Acts, Paul was before the Sanhedrin and spoke disrespectfully to one of the men present. Once the person was identified to him (he was the High Priest), Paul quickly repented to him for having spoken disrespectfully to him, for we are commanded not to speak disrespectfully of leadership.[1]

We may need to repent of how we have disrespected those in leadership over us. Whether we like them or not, agree with them or not, they still deserve respect and honor.

As we learn to utilize our crowns in placing Godly crowns on those who have yet to surrender their lives to the Father, we will see shifts in our attitudes and activities.

Another thing we need to understand in our intercession at this level is that we may not be privy to some things. Heaven only entrusts certain information to those who will guard it appropriately. Do not be surprised if something is greyed out so you cannot see it. Trust the processes of the Lord in these matters.

This revelation is unfolding as we speak, so as we learn new things, they will be added to the materials we present. Enjoy the ride!

―――― ∞ ――――

---

[1] Acts 22:30-23:5

Chapter 1
Your Crown of Authority

As we engaged Heaven this day, Ezekiel presented himself. It was as if he were in a movie, and he leaned out of the screen and told us he was part of the storyline.[2]

Stephanie asked, "What is the storyline today?" She began to see a great battle and realized it was a cosmic one. They showed her the background. She could see different cosmic dimensions, and Ezekiel stood in front of what we would view as a brightly lit star. He took his sword and pierced it. It was the Bright and Morning Star. As he did so, a liquid poured forth that appeared pure in its form, with gold and white elements flowing out. As it poured out, the star seemed to collapse.

---

[2] This chapter taken from *Embracing Your Crown of Authority* by Dr. Ron M. Horner, LifeSpring Publishing (2025)

Ezekiel moved up to a host of other angels that Stephanie began to see. There were millions and millions of angels. She realized that the liquid pouring from the star was falling onto the earth and into the crowns on their heads. As the last drops of liquid from the star fell onto the Earth, they covered the entire planet. She could hear a shout that the angels had shouted as they came full force towards the earth. She could see them piercing the atmosphere as they fought in the heavens. She could see from the perspective on earth that we, the sons, with these crowns filled with oil—this light and gold—had our hands outstretched, and we were praying and speaking to the atmosphere with authority, as if the words we spoke empowered the angels.

Stephanie asked, "What is this about?"

Lady Wisdom (who had joined us) said, "These crowns are vessels upon your heads. The crowns—they are vessels. Supernatural outpourings go *into* these crowns that are upon your heads. Each one is unique to the individual."

Stephanie commented, "I am seeing that although we may have crowns with the same name, what is poured out to the individual and upon their head, filling this crown, is unique to that individual. Will you give me clarity, Ezekiel, on this picture I am seeing? At the beginning of this engagement, I heard you say, 'Great War.' I thought it was the war before humans were put on the earth, but it's not."

The Spirit of Wisdom came up beside her and took her by her left hand. Stephanie said, "Wisdom, tell me and help me understand what this picture represents."

Wisdom replied, "This is the picture of the uniqueness of each crown. The outpouring and the infilling of Jesus into the crown. Just as unique as the relationship each has with the Trinity, so is the uniqueness of what is poured out to the individual.

A diversity among the crowns exists as well as a diversity of the outpouring.

"If each of you carried the same anointing, there would be no use for the body. Discover what has been poured out. The discovery is in the unique intimacy with the Trinity. Jesus, who has poured himself out, is one piece of this.

What do you carry?

View this in the aspect of the crown on your head, for we know it is not in and of yourselves, but what He has given. See the perspective from the crown. These are the mysteries that are being unfolded to the sons."

Stephanie commented, "Wisdom told me to ask, 'What is the uniqueness that I carry in my crown?' You are to ask." So, I asked the Trinity—the Father, Son, and

Holy Spirit, 'What is the unique pouring out that you have put in my crown?'

"For me, Holy Spirit told me He has given me a specific flavor of speaking that is unique to the Kingdom, a *unique personalization*. The Father said He's given me *a specific authorization*. Jesus said He's given me *a specific organization*.

"How is it unique for the Kingdom?"

- Pause and ask the Trinity: "What is the unique outpouring that you have for my crown?"
- Pause and ask the Father: "What is the unique authorization of my Crown of Authority?"
- Ask Jesus: "What is the specific organization of my crown?"
- And ask Holy Spirit: "What is the unique personalization of my Crown of Authority?"

[If necessary, pause and pray in the spirit before and after each question. These are some of the mysteries Heaven is revealing in this time.]

Stephanie remarked, "They are showing me the crown on top of my head, which is full of the outpoured liquid, and that as I live, move, and have my being in Jesus, I walk in this authorization, organization, and unique personalization; it spills out of this crown." You know how when you're walking with a cup of coffee and it's too full, and it spills over? It looks like that. This is the Crown of Authority *you* have.

"It is because it's not *our* authority. This is a picture OF authority."

Holy Spirit said, "The authority in *and from* this crown is what is unique to each person. **Every person walks in a *specific authority* that is different and unique from others.**"

The authority in and from this crown is what is unique to each person.

Stephanie noted, "Holy Spirit, Wisdom, I saw it from the place of what was poured out first from this engagement versus the crown being understood."

Holy Spirit replied, "Everyone has a Crown of Authority.

Everyone has a Crown of Authority.

"**It is what is being poured into that crown, be it from hell or Heaven, that is unique to the individual.**

What are you making your source to draw from?

Stephanie described, "I'm seeing a different picture now of the princes and the powers of this earth pouring out a vile liquid into the Crowns of Authority of those who walk in darkness."

The reason you have a Crown of Authority from the moment of your birth, it is because you are <u>from</u> and <u>out of</u> the Father.

"The reason you have a Crown of Authority from the moment of your birth, is because *you are from and out of* the Father. You are *from* <u>and</u> *out of* His original creation, uniqueness, and design," Holy Spirit stated.

You are from and out of His original creation, uniqueness, and design.

Stephanie commented, "I see us as babies with this crown on our head, and that's what the enemy seeks to defile, this specific Crown of Authority that Christ places on us at birth. We rule and reign.

The enemy seeks to defile this specific Crown of Authority.

> *If the crown can be defiled,*
> *it removes the authority of the sons.*

> *Satan fears when we walk*
> *with the heavenly anointing that*
> *is poured into the crown's authority.*

That is why I initially saw the picture of us all outside with these crowns on. We were speaking, praising, and walking in authority.

> *We are a part of changing the Earth.*

We are a part of assisting angels. We are a part of it all.

Wisdom replied, "You are kings and priests."

Stephanie said, "I'm also seeing that we can be kings and priests for the Kingdom of Heaven or kings and priests to the kingdom of darkness. For the first time, I've truly understood our authority.

"I mean, Satan fell because he saw us in the future and was crazy upset about it. He was upset about the authority that we have, more than him."

> *Satan fell because he saw us in the future and was crazy upset about it. He was upset about the authority that we have, more than him.*

Turning to me, Stephanie asked, "What are your thoughts?"

I pointed out what Hebrews 1:5-6 says:

Hebrews 1:5-6:

> *⁵ For to which of the angels did He ever say: 'You are my son, today I have begotten you?' And again: 'I will be to him a Father, and he shall be to me a son?'*
>
> *⁶ But when He again brings the firstborn into the world, He says: 'Let all the angels of God worship Him.'*

> *God never gave authority to angels like he gives to sons.*

Satan did not like his job placement—as lead worshipper in Heaven. He wanted what the authority sons had. That dissatisfaction resulted in the rebellion, where one-third of the angels fell.

Stephanie remarked, "Today, Heaven showed me all of this backwards. I don't understand the piercing I saw Ezekiel the angel did, unless that's just a picture of the pouring out of the Bright and Morning Star, showing what this glory and authority is. However, knowing that we have this authority to work with the angels is beneficial.

"What we say in the spiritual realm truly does matter, and it assists the angels in many ways. They have great strength, and they do things, but *we* carry the authority.

"Holy Spirit, for as long as I can remember, since I was little, I've had dreams, or I've heard the enemy's voice say that I have no authority."

Holy Spirit asked, "Were you convinced of that?"

"I think I was."

"Then he succeeded."

Wisdom asked, "Do you believe you have authority now?"

"Yes, yes, I do. I'll take this image with me when ministering to someone, this crown that spills out the glory, this crown that spills out all of Him! That is a good picture for me and a reminder that nothing is in and of myself, but I have the Crown of Authority that He has given me, that He is inside of."

Being led to Revelation 3, Stephanie read from the Mirror Bible:

² Awake from your slumber. Get a firm grip on what little life you have left in you. Your work does not mirror my finished work. ³ Remember, therefore, what it felt like when you first heard and embraced the word as your own. It was like discovering a priceless treasure (like a crown). Now make up your mind once and for all. Why should I surprise you like a thief and break into your space whilst you are fast asleep and not even anticipating my intimate intent; not knowing the moment of my visitation?

*⁴ Yet you do have a few individual names in Sardis who have **not forgotten their true identity and soiled their garments**. They are those **who walk with me in innocence** and **who mirror the reference of their worth to be equal to my estimate of them**. ⁵ Everyone who sees their victory in me, I will clothe in white garments and they will realize that I am not in the business of fulfilling their law and performance based fears by blotting out their names from the Book of Life. Instead, I'm the one who endorses their identity face-to-face before my father and his celestial shepherd messengers."*

⁶ Now listen up with your inner ears. Hear with understanding what the spirit is saying to the ecclesia. ⁷ And to the messenger of the ecclesia of Philadelphia write: I am the holy and true one. I hold the key of David as prophesied in Isaiah 22:22. Yes, I unlock the mysteries of the heavenly dimensions and no one can shut the door and I lock the entrance and none can access it. ⁸ I am fully aware of your efforts in doing the work of the ministry. I want you to see something. I have given you a doorway right in front of you that has been fully opened into the heavenly dimensions. Nothing can close it again. Even when you have little strength, you have treasured my word and have not contradicted my name.

⁹ Behold, the Jewish disguise will be exposed to be the synagogue of Satan. They have sourced their gatherings and accusations, but now I give them to you and will cause them to come face to face with you in fellowship and acknowledgement of my love, which I have bestowed upon you. ¹⁰ You have greatly valued the prophetic word which fulfilled what I endured. I will also guard you with great care, empowering you to stand firm in the midst of the troubled times that are about to come upon the inhabited world to scrutinize the dwellers of the earth.

¹¹ Do not let tough times make me seem distant from you. I am at hand. See my nearness, not my absence, and don't let temporal setbacks diminish your authority either. **Remember that you call the shots, you wear the crown. My crown endorses your crown. Let nothing take your crown.** He is the king of kings and Lord of lords not the king of slaves. He redeems his life from the pit and weaves the crown for him out of loving and kindness and tender mercies. ^{12} It is in your individual continual association with your victory in me that I will make you to be like a strong pillar in the inner shrine of God's sanctuary, supporting the entire structure of my God habitation within you, a place to be your permanent abode from which you will never have to depart and I will engrave upon you the name of my God. Also the name of the city of my God, the new Jerusalem that descends from heaven as well as my own new name. And to the celestial shepherd messenger of the Ecclesia, he who speaks is the amen. He's the ultimate evidence and the one who defines faith. He personifies truth. She is the very source of God's creation.' ^{13} Now listen up with your inner ears. Hear with understanding what the Spirit is saying to the ecclesia. ^{14} And to the celestial shepherd-messenger of the ecclesia in Laodicea write: he who speaks in the amen. **He is the ultimate evidence and the one who defines faith; he personifies the truth**, she (Lady Wisdom) is the very source of God's *creation. (MIRROR) (Emphasis and additions mine)*

Stephanie asked, "Who is she?"

I replied, "Lady Wisdom."

"That's why Wisdom was here at the beginning of this engagement!"

"That carries you back to Proverbs 8:12-32. Wisdom was present at the beginning of creation."

Stephanie pointed to Revelation 3:17-19:

¹⁷ As your name suggests, you are experts in justifying yourselves. You are convinced that you have all your ducks in a row. Your plumbing is sorted, your trade and economy are thriving industries. You think you're independent, yet you have no idea how bankrupt you are. Your entire economy is flawed since you're trading with monopoly money. It is fake currency. Your scales are rigged. If only you knew how desperately in need you are of someone to show you tender compassion and mercy. I mean, look at you on the outside. You may appear to be standing tall and proud in your self-righteousness, but in reality, you are in a pitiful state. You are like a crouching, cringing beggar. Your smokescreen has blinded your view. You think you're hiding in your fancy brand-name clothes, but you don't realize how naked and exposed you are.

¹⁸ I invite you to talk business with me. This is where it said the intimacy come. Let us resolve this together. I want to make you really rich. I advise you to buy gold from me—gold thoroughly refined in the fire, not the flawed currency of your own trade. We're not talking a mixture here, no draws, and from now on, buy your clothing from me, white garments, not the blended brands of your own making. Clothe yourselves completely with these, and there will be no hint of shame for your eyes. I anoint your eyes so you may see yourself in Christ.' (This is the look and see cream we have heard about.)

¹⁹ It is with affection that I address every one of you. Whoever you are, I would earnestly persuade you as a parent would instruct and nurture their children: eagerly acquaint yourselves with all that I have in mind for you. Now listen up with your inner ears here with understanding what the spirit is saying to the ecclesia.'

Stephanie remarked, "What I saw was the ecclesia. They were all standing outside with crowns on, praying."

Revelation 3:20-21:

[20] *You have shut me out in your self-righteousness, but behold, I stand knocking at the door. Oh, every single one of you may recognize my voice and let me in. I am so ready to join you for a feast. Yes, I will dine with you and you with me.*

[21] We now dine together in the throne room celebrating your victory mirrored in mine. This is my gift to you. It is on the same basis of my victory, celebration, and my joint seated with my father in his throne room. Now listen up with inner ears here with understanding what the spirit is saying to the ecclesia.

"Thank you, Wisdom, for being here. Thank You, Holy Spirit. Thank you for the picture of the crowns you gave us AND the authority. For anyone who believes they are too small or have done too much wrong, *the crown came from the Father when He created us* and when we choose to be filled with the goodness of the Bright and Morning Star. With the authority that He has given us, we don't ever have to worry about that again.

"I'm excited. As the people begin praying for this, the great mystery of the individual anointing and authority that's on their life, when they find out what that is.

"Ezekiel, what is the picture of what you pierced with your sword?" Stephanie asked.

Ezekiel replied, "He was pierced for your transgressions."

Isaiah 53:5:

> But he was **pierced for our rebellion (transgression)**, crushed for our sins. He was beaten so we could be whole. He was whipped so we could be healed. (Emphasis mine)

She responded, "Yeah, but that's what Ezekiel keeps saying. He was pierced. That's why what he did created this anointing for all the sons."

"This is your original design," Ezekiel interjected.

Stephanie remarked, "So, the picture is not you piercing this. **He was pierced,** and you are just showing us a picture of what happened on the cross. This is much more profound than what we thought.

"The pouring out is celestial, is supernatural, it is dimensional, and it's a picture of the unique authorization and filling of our crowns to walk in the authority, boldness and execution of our sonship on this earth," Wisdom explained.

The pouring out is a picture of the unique authorization and filling of our crowns.

Stephanie added, "I saw so many angels when Ezekiel pierced it, and then he went up, and he was with these millions of angels, and they came warring down upon the earth, fighting the principalities and powers of the air, co-laboring with the ecclesia.

"Thank You, Heaven. Thank You, Father, and thank You, Jesus. I ask that for every person that hears this message and they ask for the mystery for themselves, the uniqueness of what you have poured into their Crown of Authority, that they are empowered in their heart and their mind realizing that this lie that we've all believed that we have no authority is dismantled forever.

"Thank You, Jesus, that You were poured out and overcame our transgressions so we might walk in the authority as sons. Thank you, Wisdom, for being there from the beginning."

———— ∞ ————

Chapter 2
The Crown of Governmental Intercession

The dysfunction you see in society is the result of the wearing of the wrong crowns and the loss of the right crowns. To right this ship will require the work of sons of God to stand in the gap and do the necessary court work so that change can come to this nation.

Ezekiel 22:30:

> *So I sought for a man among them who would make a wall, and* ***stand in the gap before Me on behalf of the land****, that I should not destroy it... (Emphasis mine)*

As sons, we should desire righteousness to reign in our nation. Many prophetic voices proclaim gloom and doom, not understanding that the purpose of a prophetic warning is NOT so you can roll over and play dead, but rather, step into the courts and either eliminate the prophesied situation or at least mitigate it and soften the blow. So many voices forget that the mercy of God wants to triumph over judgment. Who are we agreeing with? Those who want to see good, or those who want to see destruction. Hopefully the former.

Proverbs 14:34:

> **Righteousness exalts a nation**, but sin is a reproach to any people.

Let's deal with the reproachful behavior through effective intercession. Jeremiah had some good counsel for us in Jeremiah 29:4-7:

> *⁴ Thus says the LORD of hosts, the God of Israel, to all who were carried away captive, whom I have caused to be carried away from Jerusalem to Babylon: ⁵ build houses and dwell in them; plant gardens and eat their fruit. ⁶ Take wives and beget sons and daughters; and take wives for your sons and give your daughters to husbands, so that they may bear sons and daughters—that you may be increased there, and not diminished. ⁷ And* **seek the peace of the city where I have caused you to be carried away captive, and** *pray to the LORD for it; for in its peace you will have peace. (Emphasis mine)*

We need to seek peace. We are instructed to in Psalms 34:14-15:

> *^{14} Depart from evil and do good; Seek peace and pursue it.*
>
> *^{15} The eyes of the LORD are on the righteous, And His ears are open to their cry.*

Daniel set a marvelous example for us when he repented for his sins and the sins of his father's when interceding for the Israelites in Daniel 9:2-23:

> *^{2} In the first year of his reign, I, Daniel, understood by the books the number of the years specified by the word of the LORD through Jeremiah the prophet, that He would accomplish seventy years in the desolations of Jerusalem. ^{3} Then **I set my face toward the Lord God to make request by prayer and supplications,** with fasting, sackcloth, and ashes.*
>
> *^{4} And **I prayed to the LORD my God, and made confession,** and said, 'O Lord, great and awesome God, who keeps His covenant and mercy with those who love Him, and with those who keep His commandments, ^{5} **we have sinned and committed iniquity, we have done wickedly and rebelled, even by departing from Your precepts and Your judgments. ^{6} Neither have we heeded Your servants the prophets, who spoke in Your***

name to our kings and our princes, to our fathers and all the people of the land.

⁷ O Lord, righteousness belongs to You, but to us shame of face, as it is this day—to the men of Judah, to the inhabitants of Jerusalem and all Israel, those near and those far off in all the countries to which You have driven them, because of the unfaithfulness which they have committed against You.

⁸ 'O Lord, to us belongs shame of face, to our kings, our princes, and our fathers, because we have sinned against You. ⁹ To the Lord our God belong mercy and forgiveness, ***though we have rebelled against Him. ¹⁰ We have not obeyed the voice of the LORD our God, to walk in His laws, which He set before us by His servants the prophets.*** *¹¹ Yes, all Israel has transgressed Your law, and has departed so as not to obey Your voice; therefore the curse and the oath written in the Law of Moses the servant of God have been poured out on us, because we have sinned against Him. ¹² And He has confirmed His words, which He spoke against us and against our judges who judged us, by bringing upon us a great disaster; for under the whole heaven such has never been done as what has been done to Jerusalem. ¹³ 'As it is written in the Law of Moses, all this disaster has come upon us; yet we have not made our* *prayer before the LORD our God,* **that we might turn from our iniquities and understand Your truth.**

¹⁴ *Therefore the LORD has kept the disaster in mind, and brought it upon us; for the LORD our God is righteous in all the works which He does, though we have not obeyed His voice.*

¹⁵ *And now, O Lord our God, who brought Your people out of the land of Egypt with a mighty hand, and made Yourself a name, as it is this day—we have sinned, we have done wickedly!* ¹⁶ *'O Lord, according to all Your righteousness, I pray,* **let Your anger and Your fury be turned away from Your city Jerusalem, Your holy mountain; because for our sins, and for the iniquities of our fathers, Jerusalem and Your people are a reproach to all those around us.**

¹⁷ **Now therefore, our God, hear the prayer of Your servant, and his supplications, and for the Lord's sake cause Your face to shine on Your sanctuary, which is desolate.** ¹⁸ **O my God, incline Your ear and hear; open Your eyes and see our desolations, and the city which is called by Your name; for we do not present our supplications before You because of our righteous deeds, but because of Your great mercies.**

¹⁹ O Lord, hear! O Lord, forgive! O Lord, listen and act! Do not delay for Your own sake, my God, for Your city and Your people are called by Your name.'

²⁰ Now ***while I was speaking, praying, and confessing my sin and the sin of my people Israel, and presenting my supplication before the LORD my God for the holy mountain of my God,*** *²¹* ***yes, while I was speaking in prayer, the man Gabriel, whom I had seen in the vision at the beginning, being caused to fly swiftly, reached me about the time of the evening offering.*** *²² And he informed me, and talked with me, and said, "O Daniel, I have now come forth to give you skill to understand.*

²³ At the beginning of your supplications the command went out, and I have come to tell you, for you are greatly beloved; therefore consider the matter, and understand the vision.... (Emphasis mine)

Daniel repented for his sins and those of his forefathers, and God heard his prayer. As we, the sons, begin interceding for our nation and its leaders, He will listen to our cry.

In the first chapter, we learned about the Crown of Authority we all possess. Some people have their crowns filled with the wrong stuff, but our heavenly Father is ready to fill them with His glory.

An additional crown is available to those who will step into the role of governmental intercession. That crown is the Crown of Governmental Intercession. We have examples of several throughout the Bible who wore this crown and operated from its strength. I have already shared what Ezekiel, Jeremiah, and Daniel have said. They carried this crown. Are you ready to receive this crown for yourself?

If the answer is yes, let's step into the Court of Crowns and begin the process.

Court Scenario

As a son of God, I request access to the Court of Crowns. I am requesting the release of the Crown of Governmental Intercession. I ask for the release of the authorization of this crown as it is placed upon my head. I receive the crown, the mantle, the throne, the dominion, the scepter, the anointing, the Glory, and the resources of this crown.

Thank you.

Now that you have received this crown, let the various aspects of this crown settle upon you. Feel its strength flowing to you and feel peace rest upon you. In your seated place of rest upon the throne of this crown, just allow the Father to saturate you with the anointing that will break every yoke. Now, let's put it to work.

———— ∞ ————

Chapter 3

Factors

In Governmental Intercession

Any permanent change to a government's political system will require that intercessors look at several impediments to progress. As an example, in the next few pages, I will be highlighting the U.S. President, Donald Trump. However, this could just as readily apply to your senator, congressman, governor, mayor, city councilman, or whomever. Suppose you are praying for a government outside of the United States of America. This can apply to your king, prime minister, or whoever is in primary leadership within your nation.

Before we begin our intercession, we need to search our hearts.

It is hard to pray for someone effectively whom we are critical of.

If we have been critical of the President, we need to search our hearts so that we can pray for him out of love for him and compassion for his position as President. If you don't have love for him, ask Heaven to grant that to you.

The intent of the Father is shown in Proverbs 8:15—that rulers would decree justice.

> *By me (God) kings reign, and rulers decree justice. (Emphasis mine)*

That is not just a responsibility of the President, the Vice-President, his cabinet, but to every senator and congressman, governor, mayor, judge, and law enforcement officer. They should decree justice and work for justice.

We are instructed in Ecclesiastes 10:20:

> **Do not curse the king, even in your thought;** *do not curse the rich, even in your bedroom; for a bird of the air may carry your voice, and a bird in flight may tell the matter.*

Scripture gives us clear instructions in Exodus 22:28:

> *You shall not revile God,* **nor curse a ruler of your people.** *(Emphasis mine)*

Paul instructed Timothy in 1 Timothy 2:1-4:

> *[1] Therefore I exhort first of all that supplications, prayers, intercessions, and giving*

of thanks be made for all men, ² ***for kings and all who are in authority****, that we may lead a quiet and peaceable life in all godliness and reverence. ³ For this is good and acceptable in the sight of God our Savior,* ⁴ *who desires all men to be saved and to come to the knowledge of the truth. (Emphasis mine)*

Our responsibility as sons and rulers is to see that justice reigns.

Where we have been guilty of being critical of the President, we need to repent before we begin ANY intercession on his behalf, for the Lord may not hear our prayers.

Court Scenario

I request access to the Mercy Court.

I repent for speaking against President Trump, the vice president, his cabinet, and other advisors or close personnel. Your Word clearly instructs me not to speak evil or curse a ruler. I have done so and I am sorry.

I repent and recognize that I have failed to undergird him and pray for him as instructed in Your Word. I ask your forgiveness.

Factors Affecting Leadership

Here is a short list of items to deal with in the Courts of Heaven on behalf of the president for whom we are instructed to pray regularly.

- Accusations
- False Verdicts
- Ungodly Bonds
- Covenants
- Corruption
- Corrupted Crowns
- LHS involvement
- Ungodly Trades
- Evil altars
- Freemasonry

For U.S. Citizens, look at the national headlines and imagine how many accusations President Trump faces. Many of these are unveiled in the titles of the news articles. Then, think of how many false verdicts he must contend with. Again, the articles' titles unveil that false verdicts are being placed against the President, his family, his administration, and his staff. Whether you are a Trump fan or not, how would you like to live under the weight of those two arenas? It would create immense pressure on one's psyche.

What about ungodly bonds? We must also deal with those impacting our leader's abilities and responses. The placement of godly bonds of wisdom, fortitude, courage, hope, and more would be very helpful to those in leadership.

Then, how many ungodly covenants are in play that are working against his life? These could include generational covenants, covenants related to the Office of the President, covenants against Republicans and Republican administrations, and so on.

We have discussed the corruption of the office and the seat of power that must be repented for on behalf of the current occupants. I recall that when George W. Bush was sworn in, some staff members from the Bill Clinton administration removed hard drives from the computers, rendering them unusable, rather than leaving them for the incoming administration. Those were childish acts and unbecoming of the office of the presidency.

We must also consider the corruption of those in leadership positions who hold the crowns. Whether the crowns have been stolen, lost, forfeited, or corrupted in some manner, our leaders need them restored so they can reap the full benefits of those crowns.

A further dynamic to consider is the involvement of lingering human spirits in the lives of the individuals involved and in the realms of the offices involved. What if LHSs were involved in causing the snafu where a reporter was granted access to the conversations of top-level administration officials regarding a military strike? Could LHSs have been on assignment to cause such a thing to occur?

What if you had the spirit of a deceased politician who misses the power he or she once wielded? Would they be willing to give up that power? What if someone in their former position was hosting them and was a dominant influence in their life? These LHSs need to be removed so the current officeholders can fulfill their roles without such influence.

It would not be surprising to find LHSs involved in many of the activities of the Republicans and the Democrats. The influence of these lingering human spirits cannot be ignored. Not every ministry understands this concept, but those who have followed LifeSpring are aware that we fully embrace it and regularly teach about it.

The last item on my list to consider (but not the last possible option) is the ungodly trades that occur regularly on both sides of the aisle.[3] that need to be canceled, and their effects neutralized.

---

[3] The expression "Other side of the aisle" refers to the Senate Chamber and the Chamber of the House of Representatives in the U.S. Capitol. Presently Republican sit on one side of their respective chambers while Democrats sit on the other. An aisle divides the seating arrangements, thus, the expression the "other side of the aisle."

We will give some patterns to follow in dealing with each of these items I have listed and cover these areas more thoroughly in the following few pages.

As sons, Heaven is teaching us how to use our authority more effectively to accomplish things for the Kingdom of Heaven. When accomplishing governmental intercession and before beginning any of the factors, follow these steps:

1. Firmly place the Crown of Governmental Intercession on your head.
2. Take your seat on the throne of Governmental Intercession.
3. Pause
4. Pray in the spirit.
5. Call your angels near.
6. Commission them to co-labor with the governmental angels of your nation.
7. Ask for the strategies of Heaven to be unveiled to you today.
8. Begin the work.

To deal with these different factors in praying for our leadership honors the Father and helps bring the will of God to pass. Using these Court Scenarios will help in the process of focused intercession, which we can achieve through the paradigm of the Courts of Heaven. I have been writing on the Courts of Heaven for over nine years. As sons, we have a greater responsibility and know-how than many others. It is time we put these principles and concepts to work for the benefit of all of us. Let's not waste another day. Let's be about our Father's business.

Before we begin, let me insert a generic prayer for President Trump:

Prayer for President Donald J. Trump: Sonship and Wisdom

Heavenly Father, we lift President Donald J. Trump before Your throne of grace today. We declare over him that he is first and foremost **a beloved son**—*not defined by his titles, victories, or trials, but by Your love that calls him by name.*

Lord, we ask that You remind him deep within his spirit that he belongs to You. *May he stand secure in the identity You have written over his life: a son, chosen, seen, and deeply loved by the Father of Lights.*

Grant him wisdom beyond earthly understanding, Father. *Let Your Spirit of Wisdom and Revelation rest upon him (Ephesians 1:17). Cause him to discern the times and seasons, to judge rightly, and to lead with integrity, humility, and courage.*

Strengthen his inner man, Lord, *that he would not be swayed by fear of man, but rooted in the fear of the Lord, which is the beginning of all true wisdom.*

Guard his heart from pride, anger, or offense, *and* ***anchor him in the fruit of the Spirit***—*love, joy, peace, patience, kindness, goodness, faithfulness, gentleness, and self-control.*

Surround him, Father, with wise and godly counselors—*those who seek Your face before they speak, who will sharpen him as iron sharpens iron.*

Remove every voice of deception and flattery from his ears, *and* ***tune his heart to the whispers of Heaven.***

Father, bless his family, his health, his soul, and his spirit. Lead him deeper into sonship, that he may govern first from Your heart before leading with his hands.

Let the mantle You have placed upon him be purified, strengthened, and aligned with Your will for this time.

We declare that no weapon formed against him shall prosper, and every tongue that rises against him in judgment shall be condemned, for this is the heritage of the servants of the Lord. *(Isaiah 54:17).*

We pray these things in the mighty name of Jesus Christ, our King, our Redeemer, and the One who reigns forever.

Amen.

The Factors

Accusations

President Trump has been under an onslaught of accusations since he first announced his candidacy for office. The mainstream media has been incessant. Some of the accusations may contain some truth, but many do not. The same thing happens to us. We experience accusations daily. The volume of accusations the President faces is hard to fathom. The following passage says it well.

2 Corinthians 2:11:

> *The agenda of any accusation is to **divide** and **dominate**. (MIRROR) (Emphasis mine)*

If I can get you to embrace an accusation (particularly a false one), I can begin to divide you from the truth about the situation. Once I have divided you from the truth about a matter, I have then redefined how you view that person and will begin to dominate that relationship. If you believe every accusation against the President and do not seek out the truth about an issue, that accusation will start to dominate your thinking about the President. How many of those reading this have an opinion of President Trump based on accusations?

We don't have to agree with the President, but we need to deal with those accusations on his behalf so that he can function on a more level playing field.

We follow the same pattern when dealing with accusations against him as we do when dealing with accusations against ourselves, our spouse, our children, or anyone else.

The steps to follow on his behalf are:

1. Agree with the adversary quickly.
2. Confess it as sin.
3. Repent.
4. Ask the blood of Jesus to be applied to that accusation and all the ramifications of it.

In just a few moments, you will have dismantled that accusation from having power over the President's life. You will have done him a tremendous favor, which you would appreciate if the shoe were on the other foot and you were the one in power.

Court Scenario

I request access to the realms of Heaven, and I request access to the Court of Mercy on behalf of President Donald Trump.

Your honor, I present the application that President Donald Trump is a liar. On his behalf, I agree with the adversary, I confess it as sin, I repent on his behalf and ask that the blood of Jesus be applied to this accusation and all the ramifications of it.

Your honor, I await your righteous verdict or further counsel.

> [Await the verdict or further counsel.]

> [If further counsel is warranted, follow the leading of Holy Spirit and the court until you receive a righteous verdict. Once the verdict is granted, thank the court and exit.]

Dealing with these accusations regularly would be helpful to the president and his administration. Without the accusations hanging over one's head, they will be much more able to hear the Lord's voice and act righteously.

False Verdicts

Remember, accusations affect behavior, but false verdicts can dictate behavior.

> *False verdicts declare you guilty without a trial.*

For example, a false verdict of "he can never do anything right" will perpetuate the behavior that the verdict espouses. Anyone can have an encounter with Heaven and experience change. It need not be a presupposed belief that if you are in power, you must do wicked deeds or put wicked policies in place. You want false verdicts replaced with righteous verdicts on behalf of the president because his behavior affects us all.

Court Scenario

I request access to the Court of Appeals in Heaven on behalf of President Donald Trump. I present the false verdict of "he can never do anything right."

Your Honor, I repent for the sins of President Trump. I forgive, bless, and release him according to John 20:23.

I ask that this false verdict be overturned and replaced with a righteous verdict.

I ask for Your verdict or for further counsel.

[Await the verdict or further counsel.]

[If further counsel is warranted, follow the leading of Holy Spirit and the court until you receive a righteous verdict. Once the verdict is granted, thank the court and exit.]

Ungodly Bonds

President Trump is undoubtedly affected by ungodly bonds, some of which arise from people's words, the counsels of hell, or the activities of lingering spirits on assignment against President Trump. We, as sons, need to remove these ungodly bonds and replace them with godly bonds so he can function more freely and righteously. Because we understand this concept, we should be the first to remove the ungodly bonds placed upon him and his leadership team.

To explain, I am not saying that President Trump is a holy man, but that he is a man God is using at this hour, and he can hear from God.

Proverbs 21:1:

The king's heart is in the hand of the LORD, like the rivers of water; He turns it wherever He wishes.

He will hear better if the saints pray more effectively for him rather than complain about him. Every complaint is worship to the adversary. For the empowerment of that complaint to come from the mouth of the sons should not be. Instead, righteous declarations are made that President Trump is a man whose heart is tender toward the Lord, who has seen the hand of God protecting him, and is granting him wisdom to position the nation for great blessings. That should be our declaration regarding him and similar declarations. The sons can do better than they have in times past.

In our court work regarding governmental intercession, we will utilize a recently released authority and revelation known as the Strike Force

Method. Once an ungodly bond is recognized (or a series of them), standing in your positional place as a son, take the quill of the Lord in your hand, and strike through every ungodly bond. You can strike through these bonds, eliminating them quickly. An example of a ~~strikethrough is this~~. Then, request that Heaven be invoked for the Godly bonds to be placed upon his bond registry. In honor of his position, his bond registry looks very regal. It has beautiful touches of gold overlays and lettering. Angels are assigned to watch it, so you may need permission to access his Bond Registry, or ask for a listing of every ungodly bond upon his registry. The overall information is likely too private for general reading.

Court Scenario

I request access to the Court of Records on behalf of President Donald Trump.

I request a listing of the ungodly bonds on every page of the Bond Registry of President Trump.

As a son, in agreement with Heaven, I take the quill of the Lord and strike through every ungodly bond placed upon his life.

I request the placement of godly bonds upon his registry on every page.

Thank you, Your Honor.

Covenants

Many times, when dealing with situations in people's lives, there seems to be little breakthrough. I have found that an ungodly covenant is often involved and is usually from the person's ancestors. Someone hundreds of years ago may have entered into a covenant of death, of some flavor, that has impacted that generation and every generation since. Repentance for the implementation of that covenant must be done so that the person can be free to function and live under the blessing of a covenant of life.

Court Scenario

I request access to the Court of Cancellations on behalf of President Donald Trump. I request that every covenant made throughout his generations, whether on the paternal side or the maternal side, be brought forth.

Your Honor, I repent on behalf of President Trump and on behalf of his generations for making covenants that were out of keeping with Your will for his life and that of his family. I forgive, bless, and release all who did these things. They probably did not know what they were doing.

I ask that these covenants be voided and destroyed this day. I ask that they be burned with the fire of the Lord. I ask that every taxation resulting from these covenants be lifted from off his life and the lives of his family and his generations.

I ask that you implement a covenant of life in his life and on behalf of him and those related to him by blood, marriage, adoption, civil, or religious covenant.

I await your verdict or further counsel, Your Honor.

[Await the verdict or further counsel.]

[If further counsel is warranted, follow the leading of Holy Spirit and the court until you receive a righteous verdict. Once the verdict is granted, thank the court and exit.]

Corruption

Throughout the history of the Office of the President of the United States, corruption has impacted the office and those who have held it.

Proverbs 29:4:

The king establishes the land by justice, but he who receives bribes overthrows it.

We spoke earlier of the need for repentance for the corruption in the office and its seat, so that the corruption does not consume newcomers to that office and they become corrupt themselves.

In America, we have recently seen a prime example of corruption in an office, exemplified by the actions of President Biden and his family. Why would you give retroactive pardons to someone who was not guilty of anything? The corruption of the FBI and the Department of Justice, which has made them tools to punish political opponents, has had far-reaching effects. I realize that very few administrations can claim to have had no corruption during their tenure. I mention the recent ones because they will be fresher in our memories.

Corruption, to some degree, has tried to rear its ugly head in many places, but that is not a reason to excuse it. As sons, our responsibility is to repent of it and allow the cleansing power of the Kingdom of Heaven to work in every area. Request that the angelic cleaning crews clean up the spiritual debris left by corruption and root out all corruption on every level, in every Cabinet position, in every elected office, within the judiciary, and wherever it is found, to uproot, burn out, and destroy it. We want to leave future generations in much better shape than we are currently in.

Court Scenario

I request access to the Court of Nations.

Your honor, I stand here as a citizen of the United States (adjust as needed) in repentance for every level of corruption that has occurred within the government of the United States, particularly regarding the Office of the President.

I repent for President Trump's sins and those before him. I repent for every wicked deed performed by the men in this office since our nation's founding.

I repent for their greed, for their lust for power, for their adulterous behavior, for their graft, for every sin they have committed. As a son, according to John 20:23, I forgive their sins, bless them, and release them.

I ask that angels be dispatched to uncover every bit of corruption in this office and our government. I ask that they would destroy every bit of corruption. I ask that justice would be done according to Your laws.

I ask for cleansing the Office of the President of the United States (substitute your nation's title and name) from every vestige of corruption.

I request that angels be assigned to police this office and keep out those who would bring corruption in this office.

I ask that you empower our President to resist and hate every form of corruption so that it is rooted out and this nation can be righteous according to Your design, Your Honor.

I await your verdict or further counsel, Your Honor.

> [Await the verdict or further counsel.]

> [If further counsel is warranted, follow the leading of Holy Spirit and the court until you receive a

righteous verdict. Once the verdict is granted, thank the court and exit.]

Corrupted Crowns

We also know that crowns can be corrupted, so the Crown of Presidential Leadership upon the current president must also be cleansed. The same cleansing must be done for every crown of leadership among his cabinet and chief advisors.

---

*If the crown can be defiled,
it removes the authority of the sons.*

---

*Satan fears when we walk
with the heavenly anointing
poured into the crown's authority.*

Court Scenario

I request access to the Court of Crowns.

Your honor, I stand here as a citizen of the United States (adjust as needed) in repentance for every Crown of Leadership that has been corrupted within the government of the United States, particularly regarding the Office of the President.

I repent for President Trump's sins and those before him. I repent for every wicked deed performed by the men in this office since our nation's founding.

I repent for those seeking to steal, destroy, or corrupt the crowns granted to Him by Heaven.

I repent for their greed, for their lust for power, for their adulterous behavior, for their graft, for every sin they have committed. As a son, according to John 20:23, I forgive their sins, bless them, and release them.

I ask that angels be dispatched to recover every lost, stolen, or forfeited crown, and uncover every bit of corruption in this office and our government. I ask that they would destroy every bit of corruption. I ask that justice would be done according to Your laws.

I ask for cleansing the crown of the Office of the President of the United States (substitute your nation's title and name) from every vestige of corruption.

I ask for a restoration of every lost crown and the components of those crowns in the President's (or whomever you are praying for) crowns.

I request that angels be assigned to police this office and keep out those who would bring corruption in his/their crowns.

I ask that you empower our President to resist and hate every form of corruption so that it is rooted out and this nation can be righteous according to Your design, Your Honor. Empower him to guard the crowns that he wears.

I await your verdict or further counsel, Your Honor.

[Await the verdict or further counsel.]

[If further counsel is warranted, follow the leading of Holy Spirit and the court until you receive a righteous verdict. Once the verdict is granted, thank the court and exit.]

Lingering Human Spirit Involvement

It has been our experience that lingering human spirits (the spirits of those who have died but have not yet transitioned to Heaven or hell) (also known as LHSs) wander the dry places. Sometimes, they find their abode with someone living. At times, these lingering spirits are compelled by dark forces to commit heinous acts against others. They can affect people, offices, atmospheres, and even nations.

For example, we dealt with the LHS in a young man who worked as a handyman. His father had been in the construction industry. He requested that we check his realms for any lingering human spirit and detected his father, who had died a few years prior, was present.

We helped his father transition to Heaven, and the young man sensed release. However, a few days later, he noticed he no longer had the expertise to fix things like he once did. His wife told us he no longer knew how to change a doorknob. His expertise was from his father's knowledge base, not his own.

Thankfully, he was a licensed electrical contractor, so he returned to that line of work as being a handyman was no longer an option.

When an LHS is removed from someone's realms, they can begin to think more clearly and, in some cases, discover who they are without the interference that an LHS can bring. That is why we want the thought processes to clear up and come into proper balance.

Registry Interference by LHSs

Sometimes, LHSs can be forced to file ungodly bonds on someone's registry. These can often be detected by their sheer vileness. Frequently, a lot of four-letter words will appear on a bond registry.

To remove these ungodly bonds and the responsible LHSs, we will again use the Strike Force Method. First, we will go against the ungodly bonds using the procedure mentioned earlier, then when we deal with the LHS that has been under assignment.

I am convinced that most LHSs under assignment from a demonic guard who is under assignment from a higher-level entity probably did not want to be coerced to do what they were doing. It is possible that some were quite willing to commit these deeds and may not have been the nicest of people when they were alive on earth in a physical body. We will deal with them in a couple of ways.

For Those Forced to Participate

Court Scenario

As a son, I request access to the Court of Records.

I request that the Guest Registry be opened for President Donald Trump. I wish to see the list of human spirits who have been forced into servitude against President Trump.

I ask angels to gather all those human spirits and bring them here now.

Your honor, in agreement with John 20:23, which states, 'Whoever sins I remit, they are remitted to they are remitted.' I remit their sins now. I forgive, bless, and release them.

As a son, I strike their assignment and the assignment of the demonic guards and their princes. I strike every ungodly bond that has been placed against President Trump.

I request the silver channel to be opened and angels to usher these human spirits into the realms of Heaven. I recommend that they call on the mercy of the Lord when they stand before him.

I request angels be assigned to clean up all spiritual debris.

I request that the silver channel be closed now.

I request angels to place godly bonds upon President Trump's Bond Registry according to his scroll and the will of the Father.

Thank you for your assistance and bringing clarity to President Trump's mind.

For Those Who Participated Willingly

Court Scenario

As a son, I request access to the Court of Records.

I request that the Guest Registry be opened for President Donald Trump. I wish to see the list of human spirits who have been in servitude against President Trump by an act of their will.

I ask angels to gather all those human spirits and bring them here now.

Your honor, in agreement with John 20:23, which states, 'Whoever sins I remit, they are remitted to they are remitted.' I remit their sins now. I forgive, bless, and release them.

As a son, I strike their assignment and the assignment of the demonic guards and their princes. I strike every ungodly bond that has been placed against President Trump.

I request the silver channel to be opened and angels to usher these human spirits into the realms of Heaven. I recommend that they call on the mercy of the Lord when they stand before him.

I request angels be assigned to clean up all spiritual debris.

I request that the silver channel be closed now.

I request angels to place godly bonds upon President Trump's Bond Registry according to his scroll and the will of the Father.

Thank you for your assistance and bringing clarity to President Trump's mind.

LHSs Being Hosted by Persons in Government

No doubt, many in our government are hosting LHSs. Some unknowingly, and others knowingly and willingly. Regardless, we will use a similar pattern as above.

For Those LHSs Simply Being Hosted

As not all LHSs are under assignment, they found a comfortable abode with someone so that we will deal slightly differently with them.

Court Scenario

As a son, I request access to the Court of Records.

I request that the Guest Registry be opened for _____. I wish to see the list of human spirits who are currently being hosted by _____, even those who are hiding between realms.

I ask angels to gather all those human spirits and bring them here now.

Your honor, in agreement with John 20:23, which states, 'Whoever sins I remit, they are remitted to them.' I remit their sins now. I forgive, bless, and release them.

I request the silver channel to be opened and angels to usher these human spirits into the realms of Heaven. I recommend that they call upon the mercy of the Lord when they stand before him.

I request angels be assigned to clean up all spiritual debris.

I request that the silver channel be closed now.

I request angels to place godly bonds upon _____'s Bond Registry according to his scroll and the will of the Father.

Thank you for your assistance and for bringing clarity to _____'s mind.

For Those Forced to Participate

Court Scenario

As a son, I request access to the Court of Records.

I request that the Guest Registry be opened for _____. I wish to see the list of human spirits who have been forced into servitude against _____.

I ask angels to gather all those human spirits and bring them here now.

Your honor, in agreement with John 20:23, which states, 'Whoever sins I remit, they are remitted to they are remitted.' I remit their sins now. I forgive, bless, and release them.

As a son, I strike their assignment and the assignment of the demonic guards and their princes. I strike every ungodly bond that has been placed against _____.

I request the silver channel to be opened and angels to usher these human spirits into the realms of Heaven. I recommend that they call on the mercy of the Lord when they stand before him.

I request that angels be assigned to clean up all spiritual debris.

I request that the silver channel be closed now.

I request angels to place godly bonds upon _____'s Bond Registry according to his scroll and the will of the Father.

Thank you for your assistance and for bringing clarity to _____'s mind.

For Those LHSs Who Participated Willingly

Court Scenario

As a son, I request access to the Court of Records.

I request that the Guest Registry be opened for _____. I wish to see the list of human spirits who have been in servitude against _____ by an act of their will.

I ask angels to gather all those human spirits and bring them here now.

Your honor, in agreement with John 20:23, which states, 'Whoever sins I remit, they are remitted to they are remitted.' I remit their sins now. I forgive, bless, and release them.

As a son, I strike their assignment and the assignment of the demonic guards and their princes. I strike every ungodly bond that has been placed against _____.

I request the silver channel to be opened and angels to usher these human spirits into the realms of Heaven. I recommend that they call up on the mercy of the Lord when they stand before him.

I request that angels be assigned to clean up all spiritual debris.

I request that the silver channel be closed now.

I request angels to place godly bonds upon _____'s Bond Registry according to his scroll and the will of the Father.

Thank you for your assistance and for bringing clarity to _____'s mind.

Ungodly Trades

Many in governmental positions have engaged in ungodly trades to gain positions, power, prestige, riches, companionship, and more. Some even to the point of sex trafficking. Often, bloodshed is involved in making these trades. The more precious the victim to the perpetrator, the more valuable the trade. Usually, blood is the currency used in making these trades, especially innocent bloodshed. Abortion is a common ungodly trade. One party promotes abortion, which provides the currency of innocent bloodshed for that party.

For example, someone might want more riches. They may be required to sacrifice a cat, dog, or chicken. They make the trade by killing the animal and begin to receive more money.

Of course, they are not satisfied with a bit of money. They want more, a lot more. They go to whoever was guiding them in the process, like a witch, warlock, or satanic priest, and they advise them that the next sacrifice must be more considerable and more significant. They decide to kill a large dog as part of their trade. They do the deed and begin accumulating more riches, but again, they are unsatisfied and want more.

Again, they are advised that more bloodshed is needed, but this time, the victim must be human—an infant or a small child, perhaps. Again, they do the deed and have the promised riches, but they are unsatisfied with what they have now. They return to their advisor, who notifies them that this sacrifice must be more precious than any others. It must be their spouse or their mother.

They may wrestle with this for a while but eventually agree to the terms of the trade and make the sacrifice. They are possibly haunted by their deeds but are beginning to realize that enough is never enough. They are enslaved to this trading floor and the need for innocent bloodshed.

Sometimes, the innocent bloodshed can be satisfied by sex with a virgin female. Other times, it is much more violent. Sex trafficking has entrapped multiplied thousands of boys and girls of all ages, and sadly, some of our politicians are contributing to the problem. The influence the sex trafficking peddlers have on many politicians needs to be repented of, and the strategies of Heaven be invoked to see change come.

Too many scenarios exist to develop a simple Court Scenario, but I will present a reasonably generic one from which you can build.

Court Scenario
Concerning Victims

As a son, I request access to the Court of Trades. I request the spirit(s) of _____ be brought into this court.

I request the relevant cloud of witnesses also be present, as well as the spirits of those evil advisors.

I also request the spirits of every victim to be brought into this court as well and be placed in a safe zone for these proceedings.

Your Honor, we present _____ to you as he is alleged to have sacrificed innocent bloodshed in making ungodly trades. I recognize this wickedness and repent of it on their behalf.

I repent for the innocent bloodshed.

I repent for the loss of wages.

I repent for the loss of properties and lands in making these ungodly trades.

I request that the evil entities that invoked these wicked trades be judged in this court today.

Those who were used, like the plaintiff here today, were deceived. We forgive them of every sin. We forgive, bless, and release them.

We ask that their corrupted Crown of Authority be cleansed, emptied of every vile thing, and made pure by Your hand.

On behalf of the victims, I request the restoration to the lives and bloodlines of the victims of these atrocious acts.

I ask angels to gather and bring those whose spirits have not transitioned to Heaven into this court.

We forgive you of every sin. I ask angels to open the silver channel and usher you to the presence of Jesus. I recommend you call upon His mercy when you stand before Him. Begin your destiny in Heaven.

We ask angels to cleanse the realms of these present from all wickedness.

We now close the silver channel.

Ungodly Trades Relating to Legislation

It would probably shock us to learn how many backroom deals, secret handshakes, blackmail, and coercion have occurred in our national political arena. As sons, let's take our governing position and legislate from the Courts of Heaven.

What many of us don't realize (and this will apply to your home, your workplace, your school and other arenas) that once you, as a son, recognize the authority you carry and that God has placed you strategically where you are, you will be able to step into a whole new level of authority and effectiveness in the Kingdom. You may be the lowest person in your workplace hierarchy, but by recognizing who you are, you become the reigning spiritual authority in that workplace. From that position, you can begin to govern in righteous ways in your workplace. This applies to every other place as well.

Court Scenario
Concerning Legislation

As a son, I request access to the Court of Trades. I request the spirit(s) of _____ be brought into this court.

I also request that the relevant cloud of witnesses be present, as well as the spirits of those evil advisors.

I also request the spirits of every victim to be brought into this court as well and be placed in a safe zone for these proceedings.

I request the paperwork regarding every ungodly or unrighteous trade be brought forth and presented in this courtroom.

I request the cancellation of every ungodly or unrighteous trade.

I request a cancellation of every benefit of these ungodly trades.

Where those involved in this trade did so unrighteously, we forgive them, bless them, and release them.

We ask Holy Spirit to convict them of sin, righteousness, and justice.[4]

I await your verdict or further counsel, Your Honor.

> [Await the verdict or further counsel.]

> [If further counsel is warranted, follow the leading of Holy Spirit and the court until you receive a righteous verdict. Once the verdict is granted, thank the court and exit.]

> [If innocent bloodshed was involved in the trade}

I request the cancellation of every ungodly or unrighteous trade.

Your Honor, we present _____ to you as he is alleged to have sacrificed innocent bloodshed in making ungodly trades. I recognize this wickedness and repent of it on their behalf.

---

[4] John 16:8-11

I repent for the innocent bloodshed. I repent for the loss of wages. I repent for the loss of properties and lands in making these ungodly trades.

I request that the evil entities that invoked these wicked trades be judged in this court today.

Those who were used, like the plaintiff here today, were deceived. We forgive them of every sin. We forgive, bless, and release them.

We ask that their corrupted Crown of Authority be cleansed, emptied of every vile thing, and made pure by Your hand.

On behalf of the victims, I request the restoration to the lives and bloodlines of the victims of these atrocious acts.

I ask angels to gather and bring those whose spirits have not transitioned to Heaven into this court.

We forgive you of every sin. I ask angels to open the silver channel and usher you to the presence of Jesus. I recommend you call upon His mercy when you stand before Him. Begin your destiny in Heaven.

We ask angels to cleanse the realms of these present from all wickedness.

We now close the silver channel.

We may not hold an official or elected position, but we have the authority of Heaven to pray for kings and all those in authority. These are our instructions from 1 Timothy 2:1-4:

> *¹ Therefore I exhort first of all that* **supplications, prayers, intercessions,** *and giving of thanks be made for all men,* ² **for kings and all who are in authority, that we may lead a quiet and peaceable life in all godliness and reverence.** *³ For this is good and acceptable in the sight of God our Savior,* ⁴ **who desires all men to be saved** *and to* **come to the knowledge of the truth.** *(Emphasis mine)*

Our motivation is to lead a quiet and peaceful life in godliness and reverence.

The Passion Translation says it this way on 1 Timothy 2:1-4:

> *¹ Most of all, I'm writing to encourage you to pray with gratitude to God.* **Pray for all men with all forms of prayers and requests as you intercede** *with intense passion.* ² And **pray for every political leader and representative,** *so that we would* **be able to live tranquil, undisturbed lives, as we worship the awe-inspiring God with pure hearts.** ³ **It is pleasing to our Savior-God to pray for them.**
>
> ⁴ *He longs for everyone* **to embrace his life** *and* **return to the full knowledge of the truth.** *(Emphasis mine)*

Evil Altars

The erection of evil altars often occurs to create a platform for ungodly sacrifices and covenants to be settled. At these altars, people would worship the deity it was erected to and make ungodly trades to appease the god. This occurred many times in the Old Testament; the instruction to dismantle them was to destroy them. The prophets would sometimes tear them down piece by piece. Often, these are now spiritual places that have been erected, rather than actual physical altars. For their removal, repentance is required.

In the past, child sacrifice has been used to further the agendas of various political leaders. Bloodshed is a currency of hell that Satan convinces ungodly, misguided people to utilize to accomplish wicked things.

Court Scenario

I request access to the Court of Cancellations on behalf of President Donald Trump. I ask that every evil altar be brought forward into this court, along with the altar attendant(s).

Your Honor, I repent on behalf of President Trump and his generations for erecting altars that were out of keeping with Your will for his life and that of his family. I forgive, bless, and release all who did these things. They may not have known what they were doing.

I ask that these altars be dismantled and destroyed this day. I ask that they be burned with the fire of the Lord. I ask that every taxation resulting from these evil altars be lifted from off his life and the lives of his family and his generations.

I ask that you implement a covenant of life in his life and on behalf of him and those related to him by blood, marriage, adoption, civil, or religious covenant.

I await your verdict or further counsel, Your Honor.

> [Await the verdict or further counsel.]
>
> [If further counsel is warranted, follow the leading of Holy Spirit and the court until you receive a righteous verdict. Once the verdict is granted, thank the court and exit.]

Freemasonry

Embedded in the founding of the United States of America is the false religion of Freemasonry. Although Freemasons deny being a religion or a secret society, they are both. They have creeds, initiation rites, their Bible, they observe a ritual of communion, they have members, and they seek to indoctrinate others into their religion. They even have evangelists whose job is to spread the news of Freemasonry.

Freemasonry is a pagan religion whose endgame is the worship of Lucifer. Although that, too, is denied.

Their constitution and creeds outline these facts. Their gospel is a message of good works on the surface. Oaths bind them to one another and the furtherance of their message and methodology. They believe their law to be superior to any other law, even the laws of this nation, and more tragically, the laws of God.

Repentance must be done for those who have engaged in this form of pagan worship. I refer to it as pagan worship with a suit. If you or anyone in your lineage has been involved in any way, I have two recommendations for you to undertake immediately:

1. Read through my book *Overcoming the False Verdicts of Freemasonry: Fourth Edition*[5] and go through each court scenario,
2. Read my book and work your way through the court scenarios of *Freedom from Mithraism: Second Edition*.[6]

Everyone is impacted by Freemasonry and Mithraism (an ancient pagan religion) that has infected the church through the acts of Constantine, the former emperor.

You cannot cast out what you have in common. Deal with it in your lineage or avoid doing court work until

---

[5] Available from ronhorner.com. LifeSpring Publishing (2025).

[6] LifeSpring Publishing (2021).

you have dealt with it in your life and in your generations.

To provide a court scenario for Freemasonry could take up the entire volume of this book. Utilize the principles and court scenarios of my book *Overcoming the False Verdicts of Freemasonry*.

Other factors may arise in the future, but this gives some thoughts on areas to cover when interceding for those in authority over our lives. As Holy Spirit unveils other factors, implement them as a son in obedience to Heavenly Father. Let's involve Heaven in our government on a whole new level.

———— ∞ ————

Chapter 4
Directive to the Sons

The following instructions were given to me just a few days after the November 2024 election. Then, a few weeks later, a portal of understanding about crowns opened, and the results are within the pages of this book and the other four books I have written on aspects of crowns since the end of February. It is now early April, and more books are in progress. The revelation flow is like drinking from a fire hose. The revelation keeps coming. Father said to me recently:

> *The sons are to govern. This is not a time for the church to lie down and nap. That happened four years ago because of assumptions concerning the prophetic—that if a thing is prophesied, it will come to pass regardless of other considerations. That is rarely the case. Most prophecies contain human involvement. The church does not know how to respond to the*

prophetic words given. Most are conditional on the cooperation of certain parties.

My sons have been given four years to mature in these matters. Hopefully, they will not become slothful during this time. It is a time to rebuild the nation economically and in other ways. Great wisdom is needed in this time.

Some have postured themselves as part of President-Elect Donald Trump's administration, but have no business being involved. They are saboteurs and spoilers. Stand with him and bless him, his family, and his administration.

Commission angels to stop those who would make it difficult for the incoming personnel to do their job effectively. Stop the destruction of documents (in every form) that the current administration would seek to have destroyed because of what it entails.

Cut off the activities of those who, in nefarious ways, would cause harm and seek to jail President-Elect Donald Trump for alleged crimes that are not crimes, but expressions of jealousy and hatred.

Release balms of healing to the nation. Speak peace to the country just as you have been for the last few years.

Release strength to Mrs. Trump. She needs angelic assistance, and her angels need shoring up, as do President Trump's angelic entourage. The angelic participation will be of great value in the days, months, and years to come. Their angels need backup. On their behalf, request backup angels to assist while their angels are in recovery. Do this on their behalf.

Call for the revelation of President Donald Trump's enemies' secret dealings. Commission angels to undo the stonewalling of justice by certain ones connected to the current administration.

A comprehensive cleansing of the seats needs to become widespread on the national, state, and local levels. A significant amount of corruption has been uncovered in the last few years, which must be addressed and curtailed. Court work can see that done.

Begin to pray for the arising of the men and women I want in positions of authority in the next election cycle to be prepared and protected. Spoilers who seek to entrap those surrounding President Trump and his future administration exist. Supernatural wisdom and cunning need to be put in place by President Trump and his closest advisors.

He needs to be open to the voices of the sons who have great wisdom to share with him.

He needs more wisdom now than he did eight years ago.

Work with Lady Wisdom to assist President Trump and his inner circle. Involve the Seven Spirits of God. My sons can do this because they have a voice because of their citizenship.

Pray for them, bless them, and deal with the accusations flying back and forth over the last season. Let them come into power with clean slates and lifted false verdicts. Get those things undone in the Courts of Heaven. You and your team are some of the sons who know how to do these things.

I will elevate some to do this concerning things not spoken of in the press, for they must be dealt with discreetly and not become public knowledge. How you handle matters of secrecy will be a proving ground for many. You must know how to be discreet. It is vital. Remember, My Word that says, "Surely the Lord GOD does nothing, unless He reveals His secret to His servants the prophets." (Amos 3:7)

Build a screen around President Trump that only those for whom it is written in their scrolls become a part of his team. He needs no spoilers in his camp or those who would do him harm.

He needs men and women who are as bold as a lion but carry great wisdom.

Pray for Vice-President Elect J. D. Vance, at this time, that he would have an encounter with the Father—he and his wife. Pray for their children to be graced and protected during the transitions they undergo in the next few years. Much will be expected of all of them. Grace must cover them. The sons must see to that.

Many have sought this for a long season. Now, rise responsibly as sons and take your place to govern from afar in the spirit realm. Do governing things in time, out of time, and in every age, realm, and dimension. Pay attention to the call to govern. Pay attention when you are called to judge. Judge with discretion and judge with love.

Govern the voices of the media and the trumpeters who sound the wrong frequencies. Assign angels to release tempering sounds and overriding frequencies to bring peace and not chaos to the nation and its citizens.

This is the start of a new day. A reset button is being pressed in the spirit. Align yourselves with the new timing of the Lord; only in this time are you moving forward and not backward according to the clock.

Follow Heaven's instructions concerning forthcoming court work so the reset has full effect on the nation.

Call for an outcry against the foolishness of those leaving the gates open and the doors unlocked.

Call for righteousness to prevail in every arena.

Call for an end to those who oppose the transition from the Biden Administration to the Trump 2.0 Administration. He is anointed for this hour. He needs to be able to flow unhindered in this next season.

Call for an end to the frivolous, time-wasting lawsuits in the courts. Request their removal to the Court of Frivolous Lawsuits, where they can be dismissed and defeated. It is time for an end to the foolishness.

Legislate concerning the persons who are troublemakers for either the removal of the person or their influence. May every door be closed to them.

A distaste will come into the mouths of the American people concerning the incessant harassment of President-Elect Trump and those surrounding them. Let it arise, for it is time for the foolishness to end.

A few days later, I received some additional instructions:

- Keep encroaching on enemy territory.
- Keep pushing.
- Don't give the enemy the satisfaction of victory, for _you_ are the overcomer.
- Press when pressed.
- Move forward when resisted.
- Invoke angelic assistance—yours and others' angels.
- Don't back down.
- Don't get lazy.
- Spearhead efforts to deal with the accusations and false verdicts being released so they fall to the ground and die not having accomplished what the workers of darkness intended, but were countermanded by the saints. That's one of the ways the saints must govern.
- Countermand efforts of darkness.
- Revoke their right to succeed.
- Revoke their right to bear fruit in any fashion, at any time, level, place, realm, or dimension.
- The arising of the sons is forthcoming.
- Help lead the charge.
- Call for the blinders to come off the eyes of those still supporting positions that are anti-God and against the purposes I have for this nation. I have much that I want to do that will bless the nations of the earth,
- The sons must prepare the way.

- They must raise the standard and bear it forth.
- I will do wonders in the economy next year to alleviate the burden on the people.
- I will cause new resolves to come forth that will fully establish those seeking to honor my name.
- Uplift those in leadership so they respond appropriately to my instructions and directives.
- Move, move, move ahead—without delay!

———— ∞ ————

Chapter 5
Retrieving Lost Crowns

To maximize what Heaven provides through a crown, we need to understand those provisions.

- **The Crown** – The obvious representation of the authority you carry in the particular arena your crown encompasses.
- **The Mantle** – Coupled with the Anointing, this is the empowerment of Heaven for what your Crown represents and provides.
- **The Throne** – The seated place of your dominion.
- **The Anointing** that accompanies the crown. It is proof of the authorization of the Crown by Heaven.
- **The Scepter** – a secondary symbol of your Throne.
- **The Dominion** that the crown represents.
- **The Glory** – the expression of Heaven that you carry as you wear your crown.

- **The Resources** – the natural and supernatural things you will need to accomplish the mantle of a crown.

If Satan gets your crown he gets all the above.

If you drive on the highway and have a flat tire, you don't abandon the vehicle. You change the tire and continue to your destination. It's the same in our Christian walk. If we make a mistake, it's a temporary setback, not a permanent condition. So you messed up. Repent, get up, and go on. The enemy will say that you have disqualified yourself from all the Father has for you, which may be true as long as the setback is not repented. However, once it is repented of, move on. Don't even pause. Move forward without hesitation!

Setbacks that are unrepented of **will** diminish your authority, but once you have repented, the authority can be restored in full force. Recognize that the enemy uses those occasions to try to steal your crown. If it got knocked askew, repent, and place it firmly back on your head. Then, request the re-authorization of the authority of that crown. As the passage says, *"Don't let **anyone** steal your crown!"*

The Mirror Translation says in Revelation 3:11:

Remember that __you__ call the shots; __you__ wear the crown. (Emphasis mine)

You choose to deal with the setbacks and move forward. Heaven isn't stopping you, and hell CANNOT stop you! Only *you* can stop you.

Finally, it says,

> *My crown endorses your crown.*

Because Jesus wears His crown, you are fully qualified to wear your crown. He paid the price. He paved the way.

> *He bought your victory IN FULL at the resurrection.*

> *WEAR YOUR CROWN!*

If you find these things difficult, it may be that Satan has already stolen some crowns from you:

- A Crown of Fortitude
- A Crown of Hope
- A Crown of Strength
- A Crown of Determination
- A Crown of Overcomer

Let's get them back!

Where we contributed to the loss or forfeiture, we must repent, then go to the Court of Crowns and receive renewed authorization for the authority that had been lost. Request that of the court, having repented for losing that crown. Then, commission the angels to begin bringing in what has been lost and fill the capacity. That capacity can also be enlarged.

Stephanie prayed,

I request access to the Court of Crowns.

Your Honor, where I laid down my authority, or my generations did, and stepped out of our authority, I want to acknowledge that and take responsibility for it. I repent of it and ask that the authority and territory taken be re-established in the name of Jesus.

Where others were involved in the loss or theft of our crowns, I forgive them, bless them, and release them. I ask for the restoration of the crowns.

I ask this court for renewed authorization of the authority lost due to the forfeiture or loss of our crown(s).

I also thank the court for the establishment and the capacity of the promised land that have not been able to come forth because of us not governing correctly as sons, but I now understand the capacity of what I am and whose I am as I indeed take in the territory, the lands, the inheritances, and all that has been established here in the name of Jesus.

I commission the angels to bring these things from this place into the natural realm on behalf of the sons, so that I might be a good steward of what you give me.

Retrieval of Lost, Forfeited, or Stolen Crowns

You need to determine if Satan has stolen crowns from you. How? Simply ask. Has Satan stolen crowns from me?

The answer should be simple to determine. "Yes or no." If yes, which I'm sure it will be, then begin to specify various crowns that you feel were taken from you. Once you have a sense of what you have lost due to his thievery, here are the steps of retrieval:

1. Access the Court of Crowns.
2. Repent for our part in the loss of the crown(s)
3. Request the restoration of those crowns you lost.
4. Commission angels to retrieve the crowns from the trophy room of hell and bring them to you.
5. Take them from the angels.
6. Put them on your head.
7. Request the re-authorization of those crowns upon your life.
8. Commission angels to retrieve what was lost or stolen from you, from the north, south, east, west, and every age, realm, time, and dimension.

Finally, we must understand that a continual association with the victory Jesus purchased for us is necessary to maintain your crown(s).

Revelation 3:12:

It is in your individual, **continual association with your[7] victory in me** *that I will make you a strong pillar in the inner shrine of God's sanctuary, supporting the entire structure of my God-habitation within you. A place to be your permanent abode from whence you will never have to depart. And I will engrave upon you the name of my God, also the name of the city [the bride] of my God, the new Jerusalem that descends from heaven; as well as my own new Name. (MIRROR) (Emphasis mine)*

───── ∞ ─────

---

[7] A continual, habitual victory.

Chapter 6
Strategies of Hell Against Crowns

It should not surprise anyone that, with the release of new revelations about crowns, hell has been trying to strategically counter this revelation. But first, Heaven wanted us to know that we can step into the Court of Crowns and receive all the godly crowns that Heaven has designed for us. We need to repent for not picking up the crowns that we were due to have up to this point in our lives.

We must also repent for looking at a false label on a crown. What do I mean by that? Satan sometimes places false labels on crowns so that the crown is no longer desirable to us. He may imply that, "You don't want that crown; it's too hard," or "it will cost too much," or "it doesn't do what you think." He is simply nefarious like that. With the Crown of Knowledge, he was placing a false label on it (such as "heretic") so that we would not pick up that crown. Instead, we need the angels of Heaven to remove every false label that has ever been placed on any of our crowns and request that the crown's strength be restored in its fullness.

Someone cannot detect the false label because the veil over their spiritual eyes clouds their vision, and they cannot determine whether it is the title or a label on the crown. The image was of someone picking up a crown, trying it on, and then putting it down. They would keep only the ones they wanted, whereas we should want all the Kingdom of Heaven has for us.

Heaven wanted to unveil some of that, and three books were presented to us during our engagement with Heaven. The first book was *Strategies of Hell: How the Enemy Uses Strategies Against Each Crown*.

The second book was *Removing the False Labels on Our Crowns*. We need to repent for the generations that picked up a crown from heaven and saw the false label placed upon a godly crown by the veil of the spirit of religion.

Once we have repented, we need to step into the realms of Heaven and see all the godly crowns available to the sons, to recognize any false labels that the enemy has placed upon these crowns, such as the label of 'heretic' on some crowns, even those that were martyred. It was the crown that was labeled heretic, and the person had to endure much suffering. As sons, without the veil of religion hindering our sight, we can detect the false labels and take those false labels off these godly crowns. The cost has been paid. We don't have to consider the cost.

The third book was *Receiving Every Crown of Heaven Available to the Sons*. This book is about stepping into the Court of Crowns and receiving every crown of Heaven available to the sons. Additionally, we should repent for the generations that have picked up a crown from Heaven, seen the false label placed upon each godly crown by the veil of the spirit of religion, and rejected that crown.

How do we deal with this?

1. Step into the realms of Heaven and into the Court of Crowns.
2. Acknowledge that we viewed the crowns with the label through the veil of the spirit of religion.
3. Repent.
4. Ask that the veil be removed so you can see clearly.
5. Receive the crowns.

Court Scenario

As a son, I request access to the Court of Crowns.

I repent where I have viewed Heaven's crowns through the veil of religion. I come out of agreement with the spirit of religion and the veil it imposes upon my life. I would like to have all the crowns that you have available for us as your son.

I request that the false labels be removed.

I request that every crown I picked up with a false label be inspected and the false label removed from these crowns. I request reauthorization of the true purpose of this crown to be released, along with all its aspects.

I also repent for our generations that embraced false labels and viewed crowns through the spirit of religion. I ask your forgiveness. I ask that the veil be removed from my generations, and every false label removed.

I receive every crown you have intended for me and my generations with joy!

I receive every crown you have intended for me to have with joy!

Thank you.

———— ∞ ————

Chapter 7
Basic Categories of Wickedness

In my book, *Embracing Your Crown of Authority*, I discuss the seven false crowns coming from the red dragon of Revelation 12:3:

> *Then, I witnessed in Heaven another significant event. I saw a large red dragon with seven heads and ten horns, with* **seven crowns on his heads**. *(Emphasis mine) (NLT)*

These appear to be categories of wickedness that we deal with regularly.

The Seven False Crowns

- The False Crown of Deception
- The False Crown of Loathing
- The False Crown of Fear
- The False Crown of Devouring
- The False Crown of Magic

- The False Crown of Secrets
- The False Crown of Antichrist

As we understand the earmarks of these false crowns, you will see how many in the political arena have embraced and wore them in their daily lives. For some, it is quite evident that, in their pursuit of power, they have sought false crowns that would enable their rise to prominence and/or influence. However, you can have prominence but no influence, just as you can have influence without prominence. Most seem to crave prominence and desire influence, but influence doesn't necessarily mean they have a significant impact. Often, when someone is causing harm to a situation, our court work can be directed to removing their influence or impact, or both.

As intercessors, we often forget that when someone lives outside God's will, they have allowed the wrong substance to fill their Crown of Authority. That wrong substance produces the wrong things in people's lives and keeps them from fulfilling God's plan for them. Many in the political arena are outside the plan of God for their life, especially if they have embraced ideals contrary to the welfare of the citizens under their influence. We must remember that many are deceived under the influence of one or more false crowns.

Our responsibility is to help them find freedom and begin living under the right crowns for their lives. We must also remember that unless we love someone, we do not have the right to pray for them because we will pray incorrectly concerning them. We must operate from our spirit, not from our soul or emotional realm. The Father can give you love for those in leadership over your state or nation so that you can pray and intercede appropriately for them.

As we unveil these false crowns, you will begin to recognize when they are at work in someone's life. That will help you have more targeted intercession on their behalf. The more specific we can be in our prayers or court work, the more impactful the results will be. Remember, we want to see every inferior crown replaced with a Superior Crown of Heaven.

———— ∞ ————

Chapter 8

The False Crown of Deception

The first false crown we learned about is the Crown of Deception (also known as the Crown of Deceit). You will recognize that this crown is a common feature in many people's lives. Some people you know wear this crown, but the great news is that we can be free.

The red dragon gives these false crowns. He said the red dragon gives this false crown to the sons...those who should be seeking after truth—and this crown is one of deception. If a son does not govern the whispers of the enemy in his ears, those whispers become accusations, which become offenses and will divide that son from the truth about a person.

2 Corinthians 2:11:

> *The agenda of any accusation is to **divide** and **dominate**. (MIRROR) (Emphasis mine)*

This dragon is more stealthy than we could think or imagine, and that deception comes in many forms, but a primary way is through whispers. If someone takes offense, they open the door to deception and wrong actions. If we refuse to acknowledge the truth in any area, we can disqualify ourselves from recognizing the truth in other areas. Each stone in the crown represented a form of deception.

Deception is rampant on the earth, and as sons, we can identify if the crown has stones or pearls. This is a prized crown that the enemy loves to put on the heads of the sons. Think of it as a game. In this Crown of Deception, there is a stone of self-righteousness. All the "selves" are embedded in this inferior crown: self-righteousness, self-hatred, and self-loathing coexist, along with self-idolization, self-importance, and self-justification, which is lethal.

The Crown of Deception appears to be a good crown, but it is not.

As sons, we must discern. When this crown is put upon the head of a son, the wrong master is in control. He often experiences "delusions of grandeur and thinks he is more right than anyone else. This form of self-righteousness is wicked; it will do anything to "stay right." If you haven't already, you will be presented with people who have this inferior crown.

Only the Superior Crowns can trump this crown, as it is a delusion of grandeur. Many will not want to relinquish this crown until they're honest with themselves and the Father.

Many prophets wear this inferior crown.

They begin to think they are infallible and are certainly not to be questioned.

The basis of this crown is pride.

This is a crown a narcissist wears, as well as the deeply wounded person. You will often find it on the heads of those who walk in orphanhood—not knowing their father.

How do we minister regarding this? What are the steps in the process?"

We must walk in humility—not grandiosity.

Galatians 6:1:

> *Brethren, if a man is overtaken in any trespass, you who are spiritual restore such a one in a spirit of gentleness, considering yourself lest you also be tempted.*

Those who wear this crown lack humility. The sons must walk in humility, as peace will be their umpire.

Those who wear this crown have no peace. Everyone who wears this crown *is looking for acceptance.* How many politicians have we seen who are broken and looking for acceptance? We have recently seen this demonstrated in the lives of some politicians.

The desire for acceptance makes people susceptible to this crown.

However, when we minister to people with this crown, we must remember that humility is the key.

Many generations bowed their knees to this dragon, this dragon of pride, and were given great understanding—false wisdom. Again...

Humility is the key.

When working with someone, often, if they are wearing an inferior crown, they may not realize that it needs to be removed.

Self-striving is involved. Remember, all the "selves" are embodied in this crown. A key to humility is a contrite heart. Contriteness is to show remorse. Many who follow LifeSpring have family members who wear this Crown of Deception. Repentance work is key. The Superior Crown of Love is the exchange. You must have remorse for improper or objectionable behavior. Some scriptures talk about contriteness:

Psalm 34:18:

*The Lord is near to those who have a **broken heart** and saves (deliver) such as have a contrite spirit. (Emphasis mine)*

Isaiah 57:15:

*The high and lofty one who lives in eternity, the Holy One, says this: 'I live in the high and holy place with those whose spirits are **contrite and humble**. I restore the crushed spirit of the humble and revive the courage of those with repentant hearts.' (NLT) (Emphasis mine)*

And then Isaiah 66:2:

*My hands have made both heaven and earth; they and everything in them are mine. I, the LORD, have spoken! 'I will bless those **who have humble and contrite hearts**, who tremble at my word.' (NLT) (Emphasis mine)*

Those that come to you are looking for answers. You must address the pride. If you don't have a fear of the Lord operating in your life, you will gladly wear these false crowns. The enemy would love to give you these crowns. Remember that the enemy is all about providing false solutions in our lives.

A rejection of truth on any level can set you up to receive a false Crown of Deceit.

How to bring people to freedom who have found themselves wearing this crown:

To bring people to freedom who have found themselves wearing this crown, remember that humility on your part and the part of the other party is key. We must let peace be our umpire, not the accolades of those around us. We must be willing to repent and forgive. We must have remorse for our improper behavior. Having a fear of the Lord in our lives makes us much more willing to do this. We must own our pride. Many politicians have pride as a significant issue. If any of us thinks we are solely responsible for our success, we are self-deceived. We are what we are by the Father's grace upon our lives.

Removing a False Crown of Deception

1. Repent for embracing the Crown of Deception out of my brokenness, arrogance, and pride.
2. Repent for every vestige of pride, arrogance, or brokenness in your life.
3. Remove the false crown from your head.
4. Ask for the Crown of Humility in its place and the Crown of Righteousness.

Generational False Crowns

Sometimes, these false crowns are passed down from generation to generation. You want that false crown removed from your generational line. Repent for those in your generational line who embraced the Crown of Deceit out of their brokenness, arrogance, and pride. Repent for any vestiges of pride, arrogance, or brokenness in your own life. Remove the inferior crown from your head and the crown on your generational line, and ask for the Crown of Humility in its place *and* the Crown of Righteousness.

Removal of a Generational False Crown

1. Repent for those in your generational line who have embraced the Crown of Deceit due to their brokenness, arrogance, and pride.
2. Repent for any vestiges of pride, arrogance, or brokenness in your own life.
3. Remove the crown from your head and the crown on your generational line.
4. Ask for the Crown of Humility in its place, as well as the Crown of Righteousness.

When you see someone experiencing delusions of grandeur, look for this crown. Only the Superior Crowns trump this crown as it is a delusion of grandeur.

Remember, humility provides protection from these false crowns.

As Psalm 100:3 says:

> *Know that the LORD, He is God;* ***it is He who has made us, and not we ourselves;*** *we are His people and the sheep of His pasture. (Emphasis mine)*

Personal Court Case for the Removal of the False Crown of Deception

Father, we ask to enter the realms of Heaven through Jesus. I invite the Seven Spirits of God and the angels. I ask to enter the Court of Mercy.

I request that You bring into this Court everyone in our generations, both mother and Father's side, as well as those related to us by blood, marriage, adoption, civil or religious covenants, all the way from your hand in the Garden and all the way forward as far as it needs to go, as well as my cloud of witnesses.

I request that the accuser of the brethren be brought into this Court. Your Honor, I agree with the adversary that I and my generations have picked up this false Crown of Deception through pride, arrogance, lies, delusions of grandeur, false humility, and through all of the selves. I repent for every self-deception that we have accepted and traded with. I repent for self-idolization, and I repent where we have been unteachable. I repent for self-promotion and self-striving instead of being led by Holy Spirit.

Father, I repent for deceiving others and allowing this crown to rest upon their heads. I agree with the adversary that we have all been guilty of this. I repent for allowing the false mantle to fall and where we were glad to wear it proudly.

I repent for hearing Your voice speaking to us to remove it, and instead, we agreed to hang onto it tightly. I repent for not taking the keys of the Kingdom of Heaven and closing these doors, realms, gates, and bridges. I repent where You have allowed us to use the key of humility to close these doors forever, and instead, we rebelled. I repent for the dishonor we brought upon ourselves, others, and You, Lord, for wearing this Crown of Deception, agreeing with delusions of grandeur, and thinking of ourselves more highly than we ought to.

I repent for being distracted by this false Crown of Deception and allowing its deception to draw us further and further away from the truth. I repent for being awestruck by the illusion of this crown. I repent for the throne, the altar of worship, where we have worshipped ourselves, worshipped what we have accomplished, and even the pain in our thoughts and minds.

I ask that the angels come and take this altar, this throne, and the idols upon it, which are all of our self's. I repent for using this crown and every gray and black stone representing the self's. I repent for where we have pride and present the crown, the throne, and the mantle to this court for judgment.

I ask that the angels bring every spirit associated with and assigned to this crown into the court for judgment. I now turn to our generations and forgive, bless, and release you for participating in this crown. I forgive them for perpetuating it through the generations and placing it upon the heads of others, and I repent for where I have placed it upon the heads of others. I ask for the blood of Jesus. I ask for the full destruction of the crown, the throne, and the mantle.

I request that the stain of this crown, which was left upon the heads of the sons, be removed by the blood of Jesus, and I ask that it become white as snow. I request the mantles be rent in two and torn as we bow in this court before the Just Judge of the Universe. We bow in humility. I say, 'Have mercy on us, Jesus. I ask that You walk through the timeline of our generations. Please deliver to us Your Crown of Righteousness. I agree that we have strayed because of these false, inferior crowns. I ask that You take our hand and bring our generations back to the truth. I ask for mercy and Your righteous verdict on our behalf and those of our generations.

I ask that you please destroy and burn this inferior crown set on the seven-headed dragon, along with its seven heads, inferior crowns, thrones, mantles, scepters, altars, spiritual residue, essences, and debris, in Jesus' name.

I ask that the Superior Crowns of the Kingdom of Heaven be placed upon our heads, overturning the enormity of our sins.

I ask for renewed authorization for every crown restored to us and those to be restored today in Your court, as well as the release of every mantle, throne, dominion, scepter, altar, anointing, Glory, and resources.

I receive Your righteous verdict or further counsel, Your Honor.

> [If further counsel is advised, follow these instructions. Once you have received a righteous verdict, begin the following segment:]

With our righteous verdict in hand, I speak to the earth. I speak to you that every one of our generations who stepped upon you, even those related to us by blood, marriage, adoption, civil or religious covenant.

Earth, I have received a righteous verdict from the Courts of Heaven this day. I bless you to hear the word of the Lord. I bless you to swallow up the iniquity and the egregious sins of self-deception and wearing these crowns. Swallow up every word and deed that was done upon you. Swallow the innocent bloodshed, sexual sins, moving of the boundary stones, worship of ourselves, idol worship, occultic worship, theft...every sin under the sun that Jesus died for.

I charge you to swallow it up and bless you to your original design. I bless you to see the governing sons and to begin blessing us. Begin pouring out your riches of abundance of truth and life.

I request the blood of Jesus to cover every place this was done upon you or in you. I speak to the frequencies of the wind to blow away the evil, to the water to drown it, and to the fire to burn it. I speak to you to return to your original design as the Lord had created you. The Earth is the Lord's, and its fullness belongs to the Lord.

I speak peace. I thank the Just Judge. I thank You, Jesus, the author and the finisher of our faith, for the Crowns of Righteousness and the Crown of Love that trump this inferior crown.

As a governing son, I pick up these Superior Crowns, place them upon our heads, and ask you to help us rule. I commission the angels to render these righteous verdicts in spirit and nature. I commission the angels to put this on record.

As a son, I call in the treasure lost from the north, the south, the east, and the west in every age, realm, dimension, and time to fill the capacity of this section.

Thank You, Just Judge, for honoring us and trusting us to wear these Crowns of Love and Righteousness. Thank You for helping us occupy the territory you assigned us. I don't take this lightly, and I ask for supernatural assistance and help daily to govern well as Your sons, in the name of Jesus.

I ask that all of this be done in time and out of time, and in every age, realm, and dimension, and that all of the spiritual debris, residue, and essences that were left behind by this inferior crown and the spirits that came with it be destroyed utterly. I thank You, Father, for what You did, and Jesus, for giving us authority and dominion here.

Court Case
for the Removal of the False Crown of Deception
Off of Someone

Father, I ask to enter the realms of Heaven through Jesus on behalf of _____. I invite the Seven Spirits of God, the angels, and the accuser of the brethren. I ask to enter the Court of Mercy.

I request that You bring into this Court everyone in their generations, both their mothers and their father's side, as well as those related to them by blood, marriage, adoption, civil or religious covenants, all the way from Your hand in the Garden and all the way forward as far as it needs to go, as well as their cloud of witnesses.

Your Honor, I agree with the adversary that they and their generations have picked up this false Crown of Deception through pride, arrogance, lies, delusions of grandeur, false humility, and all of the selves. I repent for every self-deception that they have accepted and traded with. I repent for self-idolization, and I repent where they have been unteachable. I repent for self-promotion and self-striving instead of being led by Holy Spirit by them and their generations.

Father, I repent for where they deceived others and for allowing this crown to rest upon their heads. I agree with the adversary that they have all been guilty of this. I repent for allowing the false mantle to fall, and for wearing it proudly.

I repent for when they heard Your voice speaking to them to remove it, and instead, they agreed to hang onto it tightly. I repent for them not taking the keys of the Kingdom of Heaven and closing these doors, realms, gates, and bridges. I repent where you've allowed them to use the key of humility to close these doors forever, and instead, they rebelled. I repent for the dishonor they brought upon themselves, others, and you, Lord, for wearing this Crown of Deception, agreeing with delusions of grandeur, and thinking of themselves more highly than they ought to.

I repent for their distraction by this Crown of Deception and for allowing its deception to draw them further from the truth. I repent for them being awestruck with the illusion of this crown.

I repent for the throne, the altar of worship, where they have worshipped themselves, worshipped what they have accomplished, and even worshipped the pain in their thoughts and minds.

I ask that the angels come and take this altar, this throne, and the idols upon it, which are all of their self's. I repent for using this crown and every gray and black stone representing the self. I repent for where they have pride and present the crown, throne, and mantle to this court for judgment.

I ask that the angels bring every spirit associated with and assigned to this crown into the court for judgment.

I now turn to their generations and forgive, bless, and release them for their participation in this crown. I forgive them for perpetuating it through the generations and placing it upon the heads of others, and I repent for where they have placed it upon the heads of others. I ask for the blood of Jesus to cover this. I ask for the full destruction of the crown, the throne, and the mantle.

I request that the stain of this crown that was left upon the heads of the sons be removed by the blood of Jesus, and I ask that it become white as snow. I request the mantles be rent in two and torn as I bow in this court before the Just Judge of the Universe. I bow in humility. I say, 'Have mercy on them, Jesus. I ask that you walk through the timeline in their generations. Please deliver to them Your Crown of Righteousness. I agree that they have strayed because of these false, inferior crowns. I ask that you take their hand and bring their generations back to the truth. I ask for mercy and Your righteous verdict on their behalf and those of their generations.

I ask that you please destroy and burn this inferior crown which is set on the seven-headed dragon, the dragon, its seven heads, its inferior crowns, thrones, mantles, scepters, altars, spiritual residue, essences, and debris, in Jesus' name.

I ask for the Superior Crowns of the Kingdom of Heaven to be placed on our heads, overturning the egregiousness of our sins.

I ask for renewed authorization for every crown restored to us and those to be restored today in Your court and the release of every mantle, throne, scepter, altar, anointing, Glory, and resources., and Glory.

I receive Your righteous verdict or further counsel, Your Honor.

> [If further counsel is advised, follow these instructions. Once you have received a righteous verdict, begin the following segment:]

With our righteous verdict in hand, I speak to the earth. I speak to you that every one of their generations who stepped upon you, even those related to them by blood, marriage, adoption, civil or religious covenant.

Earth, I have received a righteous verdict from the Courts of Heaven this day. I bless you to hear the word of the Lord. I bless you to swallow up the iniquity and the egregious sins of self-deception and wearing these crowns. Swallow up every word and deed that was done upon you. Swallow the innocent bloodshed, sexual sins, moving of the boundary stones, worship of themselves, idol worship, occultic worship, theft...every sin under the sun that Jesus died for. I charge you to swallow it up and bless you to your original design. I bless you to see the governing sons and to begin blessing them. Begin pouring out your riches of abundance of truth and life.

I request the blood of Jesus to cover every place this was done upon you or in you. I speak to the frequencies of the wind to blow away the evil, to the water to drown it, and to the fire to burn it. I speak to you to return to your original design as the Lord had created you. The Earth is the Lord's, and its fullness belongs to the Lord.

I speak peace. I thank the Just Judge. I thank You, Jesus, the author and the finisher of their faith, for the Crowns of Righteousness and the Crown of Love that trump this inferior crown.

As a governing son, I pick up these Superior Crowns, place them upon their heads, and ask you to help them rule.

I commission the angels to render these righteous verdicts in the spirit and the natural. I commission the angels to put this on record.

As a son, I call in the treasure lost from the north, the south, the east, and the west in every age, realm, dimension, and time to fill the capacity of this section.

Thank you, Just Judge, for honoring them and trusting them with the responsibility of wearing these Crowns of Love and Righteousness. Thank you for helping them occupy the territory you assigned them. I don't take this lightly, and I ask for supernatural assistance and help daily to govern well as Your sons, in the name of Jesus.

I ask that all of this be done in time and out of time, and in every age, realm, and dimension, and that all of the spiritual debris, residue, and essences that were left behind by this inferior crown and the spirits that came with it be destroyed utterly. I thank You, Father, for what you did, Jesus, for giving us authority and dominion here.

Characteristics of the False Crown of Deception

- In this crown, there is self-righteousness.
- All the "selves" are in this crown: self-righteousness, self-hatred, and self-loathing are together, along with self-idolization, self-importance, and self-justification.
- Self-striving is involved.
- When this crown is put upon the head of a son, the master is in control. He often experiences "delusions of grandeur."
- Many will not want to relinquish this crown until they are honest with themselves and the Father.
- Many prophets wear this crown.
- They begin to think they are infallible and are certainly not to be questioned.
- The basis of this crown is pride.
- This is a crown a narcissist wears.
- Only the deeply broken wear this crown.

- Often, you find it on the heads of those who are orphans.
- Everyone who wears this crown is looking for acceptance.
- The *desire for acceptance* drives people to be susceptible to this crown.
- Many who follow LifeSpring have family members who wear this Crown of Deceit.
- Those wearing this crown have no humility.

Remember that the enemy is all about providing false solutions in your life. That is why this false crown is so deceptive. You may think you have a superior revelation or that you are exempt from certain things in your life that are against scripture. Certain rules don't apply to you.

> *A rejection of truth on any level can set you up to receive a false Crown of Deceit.*

Identifying the False Crown of Deception

- They are self-righteous.
- All the "selves" manifest in this crown: self-righteousness, self-hatred, and self-loathing are together, along with self-idolization, self-importance, and self-justification.
- They are always striving.
- Nothing negative that happens is their fault

- They present themselves as good when underneath, they have evil intent.
- They often have delusions of grandeur.
- They may consider themselves prophetic.
- They think they are infallible.
- Do they have narcissistic tendencies?
- Are they prideful?
- They are deeply broken underneath.
- They have no humility.
- They have a strong desire for acceptance.
- They have no fear of God.

———— ∞ ————

Chapter 9

The False Crown of Loathing

The false Crown of Loathing needs to be understood. It is a great crown of wickedness. To loathe something is to hate it intensely. It is the epitome of hatred. You must delve deeply into the core of this injustice. This crown *sits with injustice*. It mandates the wickedness of injustice. This crown is the blackest of black, void of light, void of truth.

---
*Satan wears this crown
as he loathes God.*

Satan's hatred for the Father is so deep that he will do anything to hurt Him. To kill, steal, and destroy from the sons deeply wounds the Father. This stems from loathing not only God but also the sons—His created ones.

Loathing has a stench to it, as does this crown. There is darkness, but a sense of belonging comes with this crown. The belief system to loathe something so deeply gives a sense of belonging that is false and in great error in every way.

The throne that accompanies this crown is a seat of wickedness and iniquity. Those who sit upon it sit in darkness in this life and the next.

Hatred is vile. Hatred is devoid of love. This crown loathes love and anything that love brings. You will find that you may face opposition when working against this crown, as you are operating out of love, and it loathes anything that operates out of love.

Hatred consumes. It consumes the innocent. There are aspects of loathing and hatred that consume even other dark entities. It is ferocious. Its appetite is enormous. The sons must grapple with enmity against God and man in their hearts.

Do not accept this crown or sit on its throne.

It will eat you alive and consume you.

It is utter darkness. That's why you must be careful with your heart.

*The root of bitterness
is the beginning of this crown
being placed.*

The beginning of bitterness is offense, which generally starts when we do not govern the whisperings and innuendos. Let love be the ending. Desire the fruits of the Spirit.

Jesus died so that no one should wear this crown, even politicians, and yet many do. With what Jesus did for us, we should never wear this crown. Some people who wear this feel accepted, but it is a false acceptance. Politicians are likely to face the loneliness that comes with their position. They may be part of a larger group, but find themselves utterly alone.

A significant aspect of this crown is the hatred. Many on the left politically wear this crown. They utterly loathe President Donald Trump, although they have likely never met him or tried to understand who he is and what he does. He is admittedly brash and no-nonsense, but in today's climate, America cannot afford someone without a backbone. Currently, we are only a few weeks into President Trump's second term, and a recent Fox News Headline had the comment over a photograph of protestors at Columbia University that said, "Loathing Unleashed". It declared what we are seeing in today's climate. Many with "Trump

Derangement Syndrome" exhibit this false Crown of Loathing.

A sign that you are wearing this crown is whether you can have a civil conversation with someone from the opposite political party. You may want to check your head apparel if you cannot or will not have a civil discussion. Are you wearing a false Crown of Loathing?

We need to look at a few scriptures and see if we need repentance work.

1 John 4:20-21:

> *If someone says, 'I love God,' and **hates his brother**, he is a liar; for he who does not love his brother whom he has seen, how can he love God whom he has not seen?* ^{21} *And this commandment we have from Him: that he who loves God must love his brother also. (Emphasis mine)*

1 John 3:15:

> *Whoever **hates his brother** is a murderer, and you know that no murderer has eternal life abiding in him. (Emphasis mine)*

Proverbs 26:28:

> *A lying tongue **hates** those who are crushed by it, and a flattering mouth works ruin. (Emphasis mine)*

Removal of the Crown of Loathing

Do a self-check first.

1. Repent for where we have embraced the Crown of Loathing out of hatred and the root of bitterness.
2. Repent for embracing offense.
3. Repent for every vestige of hatred, disrespect, dishonor, and lying in your life.
4. Remove the false crown from your head.
5. Request a cleansing of your realms from the vestiges of this false crown.
6. Ask for the Crown of Love for yourself.
7. Pray in the spirit for yourself.

Interceding for Those in Positions of Power

1. Repent for where the person(s) have embraced the Crown of Loathing out of hatred and the root of bitterness.
2. Repent for them embracing offense.
3. Repent for every vestige of hatred, disrespect, dishonor, and lying in their life.
4. Remove the false crown from their head.
5. Request a cleansing of their realms from the vestiges of this false crown.
6. Ask for the Crown of Love to be placed upon them.
7. Pray in the spirit for them.

Personal Court Case

for the Removal of the Crown of Loathing

Father, I ask to step into the Court of Mercy to receive mercy in our time of need. I request the accuser of the brethren be brought in as Ill as our generations, those related to us by blood, marriage, adoption, civil or religious covenant, all the way from your hand in the garden and back to Your hand, as well as my cloud of witnesses.

I come to you, and I repent for embracing the Crown of Loathing out of hatred and the root of bitterness. I repent for embracing offense and for every vestige of hatred, disrespect, dishonor, and lying in our own lives.

I repent where I have ever loathed anyone or anything in our generations. I repent where I have allowed, agreed with, or perpetuated the spirit of antichrist, but also where who are anti-God, where I let this inferior crown bring an atheistic mentality. I repent for cooperating with that. I repent for our hatred of the Father and those who are His. I repent for engaging in the stench of these sins. I repent for sitting in a league with injustice, promoting injustice, and being unjust. I repent for mandating the wickedness of injustice.

I repent for being void of truth. I repent for agreeing with, being a part of, and loving the sense of belonging by wearing this inferior crown. I repent for sitting on the throne of loathing with its seat of wickedness and iniquity. I repent for the great error of wearing this crown. I repent for believing the false acceptance, the pride, and the belief that I do not have to love you or anyone else, only ourselves. Please forgive us. I repent for loathing love. I repent for not accepting your love and not loving others or ourselves.

Father, forgive us and our generations, those who were atheists, those who loathed the Word of God and the truth around it, and those who had bitterness in their hearts; I repent for the utter hatred of anything that presented itself from you or from others that were or carried the embodiment of Your love or what it would bring. I repent for having an appetite for loathing and hating you, God and man.

I ask the angels to go through time, on behalf of ourselves and our generations, to remove the crowns of loathing and destroy them.

I ask the angels to remove the Crowns of Loathing placed upon our family's heads, of those who don't trust or believe, for it came from an iniquitous generation. I ask that the throne be destroyed, the seat of wickedness be destroyed, and iniquity be vanquished, banished, and removed forevermore from us and our generations. I repent for being a part of consuming the innocent and taking innocence away from others because of wearing this inferior crown. I repent for being a part of others losing their Superior Crowns, where I removed them, or where their crowns became lost.

Jesus, I ask for your blood to cover us and for those crowns to be removed from our children, our grandchildren, our mothers, our fathers, our sisters, our brothers, our friends, and our neighbors. I declare it must bow to the Superior Crown of King Jesus and the crowns I wear—The Crown of Sonship and the Crown of Love, in Jesus' name.

Righteous Judge, I ask for your verdict or further counsel.

> [If further counsel is advised, follow these instructions. Once you have received a righteous verdict, begin the following segment:]

I speak to the earth that every one of our generations who stepped upon you, even those related to us by blood, marriage, adoption, civil or religious covenant.

Earth, I have received a righteous verdict from the Courts of Heaven this day. I bless you to hear the word of the Lord. I bless you to swallow up the iniquity and the egregious sins of self-deception and wearing these inferior crowns. Swallow up every word and deed that was done upon you. Swallow the innocent bloodshed, sexual sins, moving of the boundary stones, worship of ourselves, idol worship, occultic worship, theft...every sin under the sun that Jesus died for. I charge you to swallow it up and bless you to your original design. I bless you to see the governing sons and to begin blessing us. Begin pouring out your riches of abundance of truth and life.

I request the blood of Jesus to cover every place this was done upon you or in you. I speak to the frequencies of the wind to blow away the evil, to the water to drown it, and to the fire to burn it. I speak to you to return to your original design as the Lord had created you. The Earth is the Lord's, and its fullness belongs to the Lord.

I speak peace. I thank the Just Judge. I thank You, Jesus, the author and the finisher of our faith, for the Crowns of Righteousness and the Crown of Love that trump this inferior crown.

As a governing son, I pick up these Superior Crowns, place them upon our heads, and ask you to help us rule. I commission the angels to render these righteous verdicts in the spirit and the natural. I commission the angels to put this on record.

Thank you, Just Judge, for honoring us and trusting us with the responsibility of wearing these Crowns of Love and Righteousness. Thank you for helping us occupy the territory you assigned us. I don't take this lightly and ask for supernatural assistance and help daily to govern well as Your sons, in the name of Jesus.

As a son, I call in the treasure lost from the north, the south, the east, and the west in every age, realm, dimension, and time to fill the capacity of this section.

Thank you, Just Judge, for honoring us and trusting us with the responsibility of wearing these Crowns of Love and Righteousness. Thank you for helping us occupy the territory you assigned us. I don't take this lightly and I ask for supernatural assistance and help daily to govern well as Your sons, in the name of Jesus.

I ask that all of this be done in time and out of time, and in every age, realm, and dimension, and that all of the spiritual debris, residue, and essences that were left behind by this inferior crown and the spirits that came with it be destroyed utterly. I thank You, Father, for what you did, Jesus, for giving us authority and dominion here.

Court Case
for the Removal of the Crown of Loathing
Off of Someone

Father, I ask to step into the Court of Mercy to receive mercy in our time of need. I am stepping in on behalf of _____.

I request the accuser of the brethren of this person be brought in as well as their generations, those related to them by blood, marriage, adoption, civil or religious covenant, all the way from your hand in the garden and all the way forward as far as it needs to go, as well as their cloud of witnesses.

I come to you, and I repent for their embrace of the Crown of Loathing out of hatred and the root of bitterness. I repent on their behalf for embracing offense, and I repent for every vestige of hatred, disrespect, dishonor, and lying in their life.

I repent for where they have ever loathed anyone or anything in their generations. I repent where they have allowed, agreed with, or perpetuated the loathing and hatred, but also where those who are or were anti-God, where I let this inferior crown bring a hateful mentality. I repent for cooperating with that.

I repent for our hatred of the Father and those who are His. I repent for engaging in the stench of these sins. I repent for sitting in league with injustice, promoting injustice, and being unjust. I repent for mandating the wickedness of injustice.

I repent for them and their generations who hated those of other races or classes.

I repent for being void of truth. I repent for agreeing with, being a part of, and loving the sense of belonging by wearing this inferior crown.

I repent for sitting on the throne of loathing with its seat of wickedness and iniquity. I repent for the great error of wearing this crown. I repent for believing the false acceptance, the pride, and the belief that I do not have to love you or anyone else, only ourselves. Please forgive us. I repent for loathing love. I repent for not accepting your love and for not loving others or even ourselves.

Father, forgive them and their generations, those who were haters, those who loathed the Word of God, the truth around it, and those who had bitterness in their hearts; I repent.

I repent for their utter hatred of anything that presented itself from you or from others that were or carried the embodiment of Your love or what it would bring. I repent for them having an appetite for loathing and for hating you, God and man.

I ask for the angels to go through time, on behalf of them and their generations, to remove the crowns of loathing and destroy them.

I ask the angels to remove the Crowns of Loathing placed upon their family's heads, of those who don't trust or believe, for it came from an iniquitous generation. I ask that the throne be destroyed, the seat of wickedness be destroyed, and iniquity be forever vanquished, banished, and removed forevermore from them and their generations.

I repent for where they or their generations were a part of consuming the innocent and taking innocence away from others because of wearing this inferior crown. I repent for their being a part of others losing their Superior Crowns, where I removed them, or where their crowns became lost.

Jesus, I ask for your blood to cover them and for those crowns to be removed from their children, their grandchildren, their mothers, their fathers, their sisters, their brothers, their friends, and their neighbors.

I speak that this inferior Crown of Loathing must bow to the Superior Crown of King Jesus and the crowns I wear—The Crown of Sonship and the Crown of Love, in Jesus' name.

Righteous Judge, I ask for your verdict or further counsel.

> [If further counsel is advised, follow these instructions. Once you have received a righteous verdict, begin the following segment:]

I speak to the earth that every one of their generations who stepped upon you, even those related to them by blood, marriage, adoption, civil or religious covenant.

Earth, I have received a righteous verdict from the Courts of Heaven this day. I bless you to hear the word of the Lord. I bless you to swallow up the iniquity and the egregious sins of self-deception and wearing these inferior crowns. Swallow up every word and deed that was done upon you. Swallow the innocent bloodshed, sexual sins, moving of the boundary stones, worship of ourselves, idol worship, occultic worship, theft...every sin under the sun that Jesus died for. I charge you to swallow it up and bless you to your original design. I bless you to see the governing sons and to begin blessing us. Begin pouring out your riches of abundance of truth and life.

I request the blood of Jesus to cover every place this was done upon you or in you. I speak to the frequencies of the wind to blow away the evil, to the water to drown it, and to the fire to burn it. I speak to you to return to your original design as the Lord had created you. The Earth is the Lord's, and its fullness belongs to the Lord.

I speak peace. I thank the Just Judge. I thank You, Jesus, the author and the finisher of our faith, for the Crowns of Righteousness and the Crown of Love that trump this inferior crown.

As a governing son, I pick up these Superior Crowns, place them upon our heads, and ask you to help us rule. I commission the angels to render these righteous verdicts in the spirit and the natural. I commission the angels to put this on record.

Thank you, Just Judge, for honoring us and trusting us with the responsibility of wearing these Crowns of Love and Righteousness. Thank you for helping us occupy the territory you assigned us. I don't take this lightly and ask for supernatural assistance and help daily for them to govern as Your sons, in the name of Jesus.

As a son, I call in the treasure lost from the north, the south, the east, and the west in every age, realm, dimension, and time to fill the capacity of this section.

Thank you, Just Judge, for honoring us and trusting us and them with the responsibility of wearing these Crowns of Love and Righteousness. Thank you for helping us all to occupy the territory you assigned us. I don't take this lightly and I ask for supernatural assistance and help daily to govern well as Your sons, in the name of Jesus.

I ask that all of this be done in time and out of time, in every age, realm, and dimension, and that all the spiritual debris, residue, and essences left behind by this inferior crown and the spirits that accompanied it be utterly destroyed. I thank You, Father, for what you did, Jesus, for giving us authority and dominion here.

Characteristics of the Crown of Loathing

- It is a great crown of wickedness.
- This crown sits with injustice.
- It mandates the wickedness of injustice.
- It has a stench to it.
- There is darkness, but a sense of belonging comes with this crown.
- The belief system to loathe something so deeply gives a sense of belonging that is false and in great error in every manner.
- It is accompanied by a throne, a seat of wickedness and iniquity.
- Those that sit upon sit, not only darkness in this life but in the next.
- They have no love.
- This crown loathes love and anything that love brings.
- It consumes the innocent.
- It even consumes other dark entities.
- It is ferocious.
- Its' appetite is big.
- It will eat you alive and consume you.

- It is utter darkness.
- The root of bitterness is the beginning of this.
- It generally starts when you do not govern the whisperings and innuendos.
- They do not listen to reason.

Identifying the False Crown of Loathing

- Are they filled with hate?
- Are they not concerned with justice?
- Do they work toward injustice?
- Do they hate any expression of love that is not self-serving?
- Is their hatred devoid of love and anything that love brings?
- Do they seek the destruction of those they disagree with?
- Are they ferocious at times?
- Do they act to destroy those they don't like?
- Do they carry a root of bitterness?
- Do they carry offense?

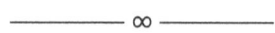

Chapter 10

The False Crown of Fear

This crown is superior in its inferiority. Of the inferior crowns, it operates quite strongly in both believers and unbelievers alike. It is the Crown of Fear.

When this crown (which is on many people) is placed on someone's head, many demonic entities come with it. They are released into the person's life. Picture how they may come in from a back door. It is a release of the essence of each of them, because fear comes with a lot of other negative things.

When this false Crown of Fear is placed upon a person, it will open a throne, and all these negative things will begin pouring out, encircling their head and trying to manifest around, in, and through their mind.

2 Timothy 1:7:

> *For God has not given us a spirit of fear, but of power and of love and of a sound mind.*

The Apostle Paul said, "I have not given you a spirit of fear," which is a specific dark entity, but with the spirit of fear comes the Crown of Fear, and the enemy distributes this crown to many. Wearing this crown brings a distortion to the mind and even affects the heart. This crown rules over many of the other inferior crowns, making it superior to them.

Many people have this crown thrust upon them through traumas. When you have trouble receiving from Heaven, there may be fear coming from the generations. You may have to remove the false Crown of Fear from your head continually.

How do we do this where we don't accept it ever again? This Crown of Fear is a master manipulator. It creates a stronghold, and when this crown is put on the heads of the sons, it is as if it tries to become embedded in them. It doesn't just sit on the head; it digs into the person's head, piercing it as if the crown were inverted.

Of course, we don't want anything to do with this crown and its ability to distort our ability to receive and flow in revelation. As a governing son, that should make you mad.

When you see it operating in the lives of others, it should anger you as well. It is encroaching on the minds of many. Many politicians are driven by fear. In the United States, the Democratic party has been far more successful in creating cohesiveness between their members. Of course, some of that is the result of the coercion of the leadership and for those who don't play along with the leadership, they will find what they do is made ineffective. They will be shut out of committees and important gatherings.

The lack of unity within each party is concerning and a topic of intercession, but as we continue, we will identify reasons for the lack of unity based on the crowns that are worn by its members.

Personal Court Case

for the Removal of the Crown of Fear

Father, I ask to step into Your Court of Mercy to receive mercy in our time of need. I ask that our generations be brought into this Court and those related to us by blood, marriage, adoption, civil or religious covenant, from Your hand in the garden and as far forward as far as it needs to go, as well as my cloud of witnesses.

Father, I present to you, ourselves and our generations, and every one of us who ever wore this inferior crown, who willingly took this Crown of Fear, who even distributed it to other people in our family and our generations, and even those outside of our generations where we instilled fear, we presented fear, where we were a part of fear, where we perpetuated fear throughout the generational line, or we've accepted it, bent our knee to it, or even relished in, or relished in it in others. Forgive us, Lord; we repent. I ask for the blood of Jesus to be applied to this.

I am requesting that this inferior crown be removed from me and our generational line as it pierced our heads. As the angels remove this crown, even though it is not easily taken off, along with every binding and every structure that would keep it upon the heads of the sons, that crown be taken off and destroyed.

I ask that the Superior Crown of Love be placed upon our heads to heal any woundedness and begin to mend our minds and mend the places of woundedness.

I ask that the technology of the Crowns of Sonship that we wear and the new day would infiltrate and destroy the technology of the Crown of Fear and that the nanotechnology of Jesus—of His love (for He has not given us the spirit of fear, but of power) and that the power and the dominion of the Superior Crown crush and destroy the inferior Crown of Fear.

Father has not given us the spirit of fear but of love, and that love is the Supreme Crown over this inferior crown, and as the Crown of a Sound Mind is placed upon our heads, that it heals every wound of the mind and that the poison that came with that inferior Crown of Fear be drawn up out of us as we are made new.

I commission the angels to clean up the spiritual debris, residue, and essences that the spirit of fear has left behind, and we receive the Crown of Superiority from Jesus, the Crown of Love, the Crown of Power, the dominion over this, and the Crown of a Sound Mind. Thank you, Lord.

I come out of agreement with every superiority of this inferior crown. I am not in agreement with it. Where we and our generations agreed and where we were lied to, and we believed that there was not anything we could do because we were so gripped by fear; that is a lie. I come out of agreement with the lie of this inferior Crown of Fear. I ask for the cancellation and annulment of these lies.

I commission the angels to capture every demonic spirit that came with the spirit of fear that came through the back door of this as it opened the door to other spirits.

I commission the angels to gather up these spirits and take them to be judged—those that infiltrated the mind and the heart, those that brought the lies and instilled fear.

Father, I ask in the Courts of Heaven that these inferior spirits be judged on behalf of the sons. I receive Your righteous verdicts on behalf of us and our generations. I ask that these inferior crowns be destroyed. Thank you for the Crown of a New Day—of your new for us. Thank you for the Superior Crown of the mind of Christ and the Crown of Love. Thank You, Jesus. I ask Father for the healing balm for the wounds. When this inferior Crown of Fear is placed on people's heads, it creates ugly wounds.

Further, I request the destruction of this throne, mantle, and crown by the name and blood of Jesus.

I come out of agreement with the master of this crown. Forgive us where we traded and agreed with it.

I ask that you please destroy and burn this inferior crown which is set on the seven-headed dragon, the dragon, its seven heads, its inferior crowns, thrones, mantles, scepters, altars, spiritual residue, essences, and debris, in Jesus' name.

I ask that the Superior Crowns of the Kingdom of Heaven be placed upon our heads, overturning the enormity of our sins.

I ask for renewed authorization for every crown restored to us and those to be restored today in Your court and the release of every mantle, throne, scepter, altar, anointing, Glory, and resources., and Glory.

Your Honor, we respectfully request your righteous verdict or further counsel.

> [If further counsel is advised, follow these instructions. Once you have received a righteous verdict, begin the following segment:]

I speak to the earth that every one of our generations who stepped upon you, even those related to us by blood, marriage, adoption, civil or religious covenant.

Earth, I have received a righteous verdict from the Courts of Heaven this day. I bless you to hear the word of the

Lord. I bless you to swallow up the iniquity and the egregious sins of self-deception and wearing these inferior crowns. Swallow up every word and deed that was done upon you. Swallow the innocent bloodshed, sexual sins, moving of the boundary stones, worship of ourselves, idol worship, occultic worship, theft...every sin under the sun that Jesus died for. I charge you to swallow it up and bless you to your original design. I bless you to see the governing sons and to begin blessing us. Begin pouring out your riches of abundance of truth and life.

I request the blood of Jesus to cover every place this was done upon you or in you. I speak to the frequencies of the wind to blow away the evil, to the water to drown it, and to the fire to burn it. I speak to you to return to your original design as the Lord had created you. The Earth is the Lord's, and its fullness belongs to the Lord.

I speak peace. I thank the Just Judge. I thank You, Jesus, the author and the finisher of our faith, for the Crowns of Righteousness and the Crown of Love that trump this inferior crown.

As a governing son, I pick up these Superior Crowns, place them upon our heads, and ask you to help us rule. I commission the angels to render these righteous verdicts in the spirit and the natural. I commission the angels to put this on record.

Thank you, Just Judge, for honoring us and trusting us with the responsibility of wearing these Crowns of Love and Crowns of Righteousness. Thank you for helping us occupy the territory you assigned us. I don't take this lightly; ask for supernatural assistance and help daily to govern well as Your sons in the name of Jesus.

As a son, I call in the treasure lost from the north, the south, the east, and the west in every age, realm, dimension, and time to fill the capacity of this section.

I ask that all of this be done in time and out of time, and in every age, realm, and dimension, and that all of the spiritual debris, residue, and essences that were left behind by this inferior crown and the spirits that came with it be destroyed utterly. I thank You, Father, for what you did, Jesus, for giving us authority and dominion here.

Court Case
for the Removal of the Crown of Fear
Off of Someone

Father, I ask to step into Your Court of Mercy to receive mercy in our time of need on behalf of _____. I ask that their generations be brought into this Court and those related to them by blood, marriage, adoption, civil or religious covenant, from Your hand in the garden and as far forward as far as it needs to go, as well as their cloud of witnesses.

Father, I present to you, _____ and their generations, and every one of them who ever wore this inferior crown, who willingly took this Crown of Fear, who even distributed it to other people in their family and their generations, and even those outside of their generations where I they instilled fear, presented fear, where they were a part of fear, where they perpetuated fear throughout the generational line, or accepted it, bent their knee to it, or even relished in, or relished it in others. Forgive them, Lord; I repent on their behalf. I ask for the blood of Jesus to be applied to this.

I am requesting that this inferior crown be removed from them and their generational line as it pierced their heads. I ask that the angels remove this crown (even though it is not easily taken off), along with every binding and every structure that would keep it upon their heads. I request that the Crown of Fear be removed and destroyed.

I ask that the Superior Crown of Love be placed upon their heads to heal any woundedness and begin to mend their minds and mend the places of woundedness.

I ask that the technology of the Crowns of Sonship that they wear and the new day would infiltrate and destroy the technology of the Crown of Fear and that the nanotechnology of Jesus—of His love (for He has not given them the spirit of fear, but of power) and that the power and the dominion of the Superior Crown crush and destroy the inferior Crown of Fear.

Father has not given us the spirit of fear but of love, and that love is the Supreme Crown over this inferior crown, and as the Crown of a Sound Mind is placed upon their heads, that it heals every wound of the mind and that the poison that came with that inferior Crown of Fear be drawn up out of them as they are made new.

I commission the angels to clean up the spiritual debris, residue, and essences that the spirit of fear has left behind, so they receive the Superior Crown from Jesus—the Crown of Love, and the Crown of Power—the dominion over this, and the Crown of a Sound Mind. Thank you, Lord.

I come out of agreement with every form of superiority of the inferior Crown of Fear. They are not in agreement with it, and I am not in agreement with it. Where they and their generations agreed and where they were lied to, and they believed that there was nothing they could do because they were so gripped by fear; that is a lie. I come out of agreement with the lie of this inferior Crown of Fear. I ask for the cancellation and annulment of these lies.

I commission the angels to capture every demonic spirit that came with the spirit of fear that came through the back door of this as it opened up the door to other spirits.

I commission the angels to gather up these spirits and take them to be judged—those that infiltrated the mind and the heart, those that brought the lies and instilled the fear.

Father, I ask in the Courts of Heaven that these inferior spirits be judged on behalf of the sons. I receive Your righteous verdicts on behalf of them and their generations. I ask that these inferior crowns be destroyed.

I thank you for the Crown of a New Day—of your new for us. Thank you for the Superior Crown of the mind of Christ and the Crown of Love. Thank You, Jesus.

I ask Father for the healing balm for the wounds, for when this inferior Crown of Fear is placed on people's heads, it creates ugly wounds.

Further, I request the destruction of this throne, mantle, and crown by the name and blood of Jesus.

I come out of agreement with the master of this crown. Forgive us where they traded and agreed with it.

I ask that you please destroy and burn this inferior crown which is set on the seven-headed dragon, the dragon, its seven heads, its inferior crowns, thrones, mantles, scepters, altars, spiritual residue, essences, and debris, in Jesus' name.

I ask for the Superior Crowns of the Kingdom of Heaven to be placed on our heads, overturning the egregiousness of our sins.

I ask for renewed authorization for every crown restored to us and those to be restored today in Your court, as well as the release of every mantle, throne, dominion, scepter, altar, anointing, Glory, and resources.

Your Honor, I respectfully request Your righteous verdict or further guidance.

> [If further counsel is advised, follow these instructions. Once you have received a righteous verdict, begin the following segment:]

I speak to the earth that every one of their generations who stepped upon you, even those related to them by blood, marriage, adoption, civil or religious covenant.

Earth, I have received a righteous verdict from the Courts of Heaven this day. I bless you to hear the word of the Lord. I bless you to swallow up the iniquity and the egregious sins of self-deception and wearing these inferior crowns. Swallow up every word and deed that was done upon you. Swallow the innocent bloodshed, sexual sins, moving of the boundary stones, worship of themselves, idol worship, occultic worship, theft…every sin under the sun that Jesus died for. I charge you to swallow it up and bless you to your original design. I bless you to see the governing sons and to begin blessing them. Begin pouring out your riches of abundance of truth and life.

I request the blood of Jesus to cover every place this was done upon you or in you. I speak to the frequencies of the wind to blow away the evil, to the water to drown it, and to the fire to burn it. I speak to you to return to your original design as the Lord had created you. The Earth is the Lord's, and its fullness belongs to the Lord.

I speak peace. I thank the Just Judge. I thank You, Jesus, the author and the finisher of our faith, for the Crowns of Righteousness and the Crown of Love that trump this inferior crown.

As a governing son, I pick up these Superior Crowns, place them upon our heads, and ask you to help them rule. I commission the angels to render these righteous verdicts in the spirit and the natural. I commission the angels to put this on record.

Thank you, Just Judge, for honoring me and trusting me and them with the responsibility of wearing these Crowns of Love and Crowns of Righteousness. Thank you for helping them occupy the territory you assigned them. I don't take this lightly; ask for supernatural assistance and help daily to govern well as Your sons in the name of Jesus.

As a son, I call in the treasure lost from the north, the south, the east, and the west in every age, realm, dimension, and time to fill the capacity of this section.

I ask that all of this be done in time and out of time, and in every age, realm, and dimension, and that all of the spiritual debris, residue, and essences that were left behind by this inferior crown and the spirits that came with it be destroyed utterly. I thank You, Father, for what you did, Jesus, for giving us authority and dominion here.

Characteristics of the False Crown of Fear

- With the spirit of fear comes this Crown of Fear, and the enemy distributes these crowns.
- Wearing this crown brings a distortion to the mind and even affects the heart.
- Many people have this crown thrust upon them through traumas.
- When you have trouble receiving from Heaven, there may be fear coming from your generations.
- You may have to remove the Crown of Fear from your head continually.
- It enables master manipulation.
- This crown creates a stronghold.
- It tries to become embedded in them.
- This crown distorts your ability to receive and flow in revelation.

Identifying the False Crown of Fear

- Are they consumed with fear?
- Do they live in terror?
- Do they always circle back to something to fear?
- Do they have a negative mindset?
- Do they exhibit distorted thinking?
- Is their physical heart having issues?
- Do they have trouble receiving from Heaven?

- Do they have trouble receiving or flowing in revelation?

―――― ∞ ――――

Chapter 11

The False Crown of Magic

This crown is unusually beautiful and alluring. It appeared as a crown with purple stones mounted on it. The stones were the most beautiful color, purple. The crown the stones were mounted on was also beautiful, dark, and larger than the other crowns. This was important because from the back of the crown to the front, the stones were all the same size except for the one in the very front. The others were all mounted on different points, except the center stone. The middle point at the front of the crown was higher and had a beautiful, long, elongated purple stone, whereas all other stones were shorter. The crown was suspended in the air, and its scenery was black.

The thing about the enemy is that *he doesn't trust anyone.* So, a larger stone embedded in this crown was the eye that allowed him to see what they did for him. It's like a back-and-forth messaging. Because he doesn't trust anyone, he sets up a monitoring system in each crown. It is wicked technology.

Although its beauty is enchanting, it is not a suitable crown. It seems good, but the good is contaminated by darkness and falsehood. This was a *Crown of Magic*. It is the crown on the fifth head of the dragon.

It is tantalizing, which makes this crown unique. It is a deception that comes with witchcraft. This crown is unique in itself.

The deception here is that many believe some forms of witchcraft are good.

We saw this culturally a few years ago with the popularity of the Harry Potter series. Years before, we were socially inoculated by the television show, Bewitched. Growing up, we were taught the false narrative of a good witch versus an evil witch, as depicted in the movie *The Wizard of Oz*. We have been pre-conditioned to the belief that there is good witchcraft and evil witchcraft. NO! It is all bad!

The brides of Satan wear this crown. It has an allure to it. It lures people in. It is filled with a lust for power. It has an elevation to it. This crown suspends those who wear it. They are in a realm of darkness that looks like light to them. It feels like power. It entices their senses, and it is full of greed.

> *It is the most dishonoring of crowns as dishonor alights upon the heads of those who wear it, for they have indeed dishonored the Lord.*

This crown has elements of truth that pull people in.

> *When a lie is embedded in the truth, it makes it a lie.*

The spirit of whoring is with this crown. It has an insatiable appetite and is handcrafted in the depths of hell.

> *Many of these crowns come through the assignments on the generational line, where there has been a lot of witchcraft.*

We must remove these crowns from their generational line that came through bloodline iniquity and sin. Then, commission the angels to go and *blight* these crowns from the generational line. It is a blight in the bloodline from which these crowns originate. To blight something is essentially to smite it from the generational lines. This crown attaches Many lingering human spirits to the generational line.

When you remove the crowns through repentance, you remove the lingering human spirits who wear them. There will be a fight about it. They're not going to want to give them up. These crowns have empowered them and were passed down through the generations. However, they will be removed.

Know that blight is something that destroys or impairs. When that crown is on the bloodline, it seeks to destroy. Remember, light dispels the darkness.

This crown also has a throne that needs to be dismantled. It is very much like an altar.

Personal Court Case for Removal of the Crown of Magic

Father, I ask to step into Your Court of Mercy, through Jesus, on behalf of me and my generations. I ask that the accuser of the brethren be brought in as well as our generational line, from both sides of the family, and those who are with us by blood, marriage, adoption, civil or religious covenant, from your hand in the garden and all the way forward as far as it needs to go, as well as my cloud of witnesses.

Your Honor, I agree with the adversary that we were deceived by magic and everything it encompasses.

I repent for magic, for the use of it, for the places in the generations that yielded to it, utilized it, for those who took it up, that felt empowered by it, that were deceived because of it, and for those that elevated themselves in believing the lie.

I repent for those in the generations who practiced magic but also deceived others with bits of truth to pull them into the lie. I repent on their behalf.

I repent on behalf of everyone who believed the lie, succumbed to it, and then projected it, and perpetuated it through the generational line.

I repent for agreeing with the spirit of whoring, for trading with it, for seducing because of it, and for allowing it.

I repent for the garments they wore. I ask that they be removed and destroyed now.

I repent, sir, all the way back to Your hand and all the way forward. Father, I repent for taking this inferior crown and for the use of this crown. Where they saw it as useful, yet it was a lie.

I repent where I put this inferior crown on other people's heads and our own.

On behalf of the lingering human spirits who are or who are not a part of our bloodline, as well as our generations who are now assigned to the bloodline because of taking up these inferior crowns. I repent on their behalf for every sin under the sun, which is egregious in nature, which dishonored and brought dishonor to the Lord because of taking up and for wearing these inferior crowns.

I commission the angels to go through the timelines, ages, and dimensions for every person who wore this inferior crown, and I commission you to take it off their heads as we stand before the Lord in repentance for them. I forgive, bless, and release them.

I ask the angels to open up the silver channel and take the demonic guard and the bosses who were assigned to these LHSs to Jesus's feet for judgment. To every lingering human spirit in the generational line, you will go and see Jesus today. You are not staying.

I forgive you, bless you, and release you for what you were doing in and through the bloodline. You are removed this day by the hand of God because of repentance, which we are allowed to do. He forgave us, and I forgive you.

When you see Jesus, I suggest you ask Him for mercy. Angels, I commission you to destroy every inferior crown of witchcraft in the name of Jesus.

I ask for a Crown of Truth to be given to our generational line—the utter and distinct truth, the Superior Crown that causes all other inferior crowns to be dismantled and destroyed, as their knee must bow, in the name of Jesus.

I ask that the thrones and mantles be found, dismantled, and destroyed in every place throughout the generational line.

Where our generations set this up as a type of altar, I ask that it be destroyed, and that every attendant of every altar be captured and dealt with according to the will of the Father, and that the idol of witchcraft, as well as this Crown of Magic, be judged in the courts today.

I commission the angels to take every spirit or entity assigned or associated with this throne, inferior crown, mantle, and scepter to court for judgment. I commission the angels to destroy the thrones forever and that the altar of the Lord be established in their place, in and through the bloodline. I request that angels be assigned there to worship and that the Crown of Truth be established as it sits upon the altar of the Lord.

I request that every false scepter that came with this inferior crown and this throne, which was considered to be a wand, also be taken from the generational bloodline and be utterly destroyed, annulled, and removed. I ask that its frequency be dismantled and destroyed in the name of Jesus.

I request the realm of the inferior hovering crown, the realm from which it came, be closed, and that there be a closed, sealed door in and upon the line of the generations forevermore with no ability to reopen.

I request that the center stone of this inferior crown, which is the eye, be utterly crushed, annulled, canceled, destroyed, and blinded forever in, through, and upon the generational line.

I ask for the amendment of 'As if it Never Were.'

I ask that you please destroy and burn this inferior crown set on the seven-headed dragon, the dragon, its seven heads, its inferior crowns, thrones, mantles, scepters, altars, spiritual residue, essences, and debris, in Jesus' name.

I ask that the Superior Crowns of the Kingdom of Heaven be placed upon our heads, overturning the enormity of our sins.

I ask for renewed authorization for every crown restored to us, and those to be restored today in Your court, as well as the release of every mantle, throne, scepter, altar, anointing, Glory, and resources., and Glory.

I ask for our righteous verdicts or further counsel.

> [If further counsel is advised, follow these instructions. Once you have received a righteous verdict, begin the following segment:]

I speak to the earth, water, air, and fire. I have received a righteous verdict, and since the world and the fullness of it belong to the Lord, I charge you to swallow up, drown, blow away and burn all evil words, deeds, lies, witchcraft, innocent bloodshed, sexual sins, occultic cauldrons, evil rooms, evil technologies, spells, hex's, vexes, incantations, voodoo, dark art, manipulation, monitoring, astral projections, evil projections, counterfeit intelligence, and all other darkness or evil done upon the earth, through the air, to the water and using fire.

I bless you to the fullness of your original design and charge you to bless us as the Lord walks through time, restoring it and you to their fullness. I do this in the name and by the blood of Jesus, and as a governing son.

As a son, I call in the treasure lost from the north, the south, the east, and the west in every age, realm, dimension, and time to fill the capacity of this section.

I ask that all of this be done in time and out of time, and in every age, realm, and dimension, and that all of the spiritual debris, residue, and essences left behind by this inferior crown and the spirits that came with it be destroyed utterly. Thank You, Father, for what you did., Thank You, Jesus, for giving us authority and dominion here.

Court Case
for Removal of the Crown of Magic
Off of Someone

Father, I ask to step into Your Court of Mercy, through Jesus, on behalf of _____ and their generations. I ask that the accuser of the brethren be brought in as well as their generational line, from both sides of the family, and those who are with them by blood, marriage, adoption, civil or religious covenant, from your hand in the garden and as far forward as it needs to go, as well as their cloud of witnesses.

Your Honor, I agree with the adversary that they were deceived by magic and everything it encompasses.

I repent for magic, for the use of it, for the places in their generations that yielded to it, utilized it, for those who took it up, who felt empowered by it, who were deceived because of it, and for those who elevated themselves in believing the lie.

I repent for those in their generations who practiced magic but also deceived others with bits of truth to pull them into the lie. I repent on their behalf.

I repent on behalf of everyone in their generations who believed the lie, succumbed to it, projected it, and perpetuated it through the generational line.

I repent for agreeing with the spirit of whoring, for trading with it, for seducing because of it, and for allowing it.

I repent for the garments they wore. I ask that they be removed and destroyed now.

I repent, sir, all the way back to Your hand and forward. Father, I repent for taking this inferior crown and for the use of this crown. They saw it as useful, yet it was a lie.

I repent where they put this inferior crown on other people's heads and their own.

On behalf of the lingering human spirits who are or are not a part of our bloodline and their generations who are now assigned to the bloodline because of taking up these inferior crowns. I repent on their behalf for every sin under the sun, which is egregious, which dishonored and brought dishonor to the Lord because of taking up and for wearing these inferior crowns.

I commission the angels to go through the timelines, ages, and dimensions for every person who wore this inferior crown, and I commission you to take it off their heads as we stand before the Lord in repentance for them. I forgive, bless, and release them.

I ask the angels to open up the silver channel and take the demonic guard and the bosses who were assigned to these LHSs to Jesus' feet for judgment. To every lingering human spirit in the generational line, you will go and see Jesus today. You are not staying.

I forgive you, bless you, and release you for what you were doing in and through the bloodline. You are removed this day by the hand of God because of repentance, which we are allowed to do. He forgave us, and I forgive you.

When you see Jesus, I suggest you ask Him for mercy. Angels, I commission you to destroy every inferior crown of witchcraft in the name of Jesus.

I ask for a Crown of Truth to be given to our generational line—the utter and distinct truth, the Superior Crown that causes all other inferior crowns to be dismantled and destroyed, as their knee must bow, in the name of Jesus.

I ask that the thrones and mantles be found, dismantled, and destroyed in every place throughout the generational line.

Where their generations set this up as a type of altar, I ask that it be destroyed, and that every attendant of every altar be captured and dealt with according to the will of the Father, and that the idol of witchcraft, as well as this Crown of Magic, be judged in the courts today.

I commission the angels to take every spirit or entity assigned or associated with this throne, inferior crown, mantle, and scepter to court for judgment. I commission the angels to destroy the thrones forever, and that the altar of the Lord be established in their place, in and through the bloodline. I request that angels be assigned there to worship and that the Crown of Truth be established as it sits upon the altar of the Lord.

I request that every false scepter that came with this inferior crown and this throne, which was considered to be a wand, also be taken from the generational bloodline and be utterly destroyed, annulled, and removed. I ask that its frequency be dismantled and destroyed in the name of Jesus.

I request the realm of the inferior hovering crown, the realm from which it came, be closed, and that there be a closed, sealed door in and upon the line of the generations forevermore with no ability to reopen.

I request that the center stone of this inferior crown, which is the eye, be utterly crushed, annulled, canceled, destroyed, and blinded forever in, through, and upon the generational line.

I ask for the amendment of 'As if it Never Were.'

I ask that you please destroy and burn this inferior crown set on the seven-headed dragon, the dragon, its seven heads, its inferior crowns, thrones, mantles, scepters, altars, spiritual residue, essences, and debris, in Jesus' name.

I ask that the Superior Crowns of the Kingdom of Heaven be placed upon our heads, overturning the enormity of our sins.

I ask for renewed authorization for every crown restored to us, and those to be restored today in Your court and the release of every mantle, throne, scepter, altar, anointing, Glory, and resources., and Glory.

I ask for our righteous verdicts or further counsel.

> [If further counsel is advised, follow these instructions. Once you have received a righteous verdict, begin the following segment:]

I speak to the earth, water, air, and fire. I have received a righteous verdict, and since the world and the fullness of it belong to the Lord, I charge you to swallow up, drown, blow away and burn all evil words, deeds, lies, witchcraft, innocent bloodshed, sexual sins, occultic cauldrons, evil rooms, evil technologies, spells, hex's, vexes, incantations, voodoo, dark art, manipulation, monitoring, astral projections, evil projections, counterfeit intelligence, and all other darkness or evil done upon the earth, through the air, to the water and using fire.

I bless you to the fullness of your original design and charge you to bless us as the Lord walks through time, restoring it and you to their fullness. I do this in the name and by the blood of Jesus, and as a governing son.

As a son, I call in the treasure lost from the north, the south, the east, and the west in every age, realm, dimension, and time to fill the capacity of this section.

I ask that all of this be done in time and out of time, and in every age, realm, and dimension, and that all of the spiritual debris, residue, and essences left behind by this inferior crown and the spirits that came with it be destroyed utterly. I thank You, Father, for what you did, Jesus, for giving us authority and dominion here.

Characteristics of the False Crown of Magic

- It has purple stones mounted on it.
- The crown is larger than the other crowns.
- This is not a good crown.
- It is a tantalizing, seductive crown.
- This crown is unique due to the deception that comes with witchcraft.
- This crown is unique in itself.

- It deceives you to think many believe forms of witchcraft are good.
- It has an allure to it.
- It's full of lust for power.
- It manifests as a realm of darkness that looks like light to them.
- It feels like power.
- It entices their senses.
- It is full of greed.
- It is the most dishonoring of crowns as dishonor alights upon the heads of those that wear it, for they have indeed dishonored the Lord.
- This crown contains elements of truth that pull people in.
- The spirit of whoring is with this crown.
- It has an insatiable appetite and is handcrafted in hell.
- Many of these crowns come through the assignments on the generational line, where there has been a lot of witchcraft.
- Many lingering human spirits are on the generational line because of this crown.
- It is a blight that destroys and impairs.
- This crown also has a throne that needs to be dismantled. It is very much like an altar.
- There is a throne associated with this crown; it is a seat of its power.
- It is embedded in distrust.
- He uses the main stone as a monitoring system.
- It is wicked technology.

Identifying the False Crown of Magic

- Have they embraced Harry Potter and other forms of witchcraft that they have no problem with?
- Is greed a problem with them?
- Do they have sexual issues?
- Do they have problems with lingering human spirits?
- Are they distrustful?
- Do they have an insatiable appetite for things?

———— ∞ ————

Chapter 12

The False Crown of Secrets

This inferior crown is unlike any other. It is quiet and stealthy. It silences the sons. It is bloodthirsty, and it screams of desire to pierce frequencies and it walks with the spirit of death. Its inner workings are harlotry, divination, and mockery.

The sounds of intercession rub and excoriate the head of this dragon, which was why it seeks to silence the sons. The Pharisees wore this crown with their lofty robes. Violence comes from the mouth of this dragon who wears this crown.

This false Crown of Secrets works with the false Crown of Antichrist. This dragon's head has a cloak around it to make it hidden.

---

*This is the seat of Freemasonry,
so it has a throne.
It is shrouded in secrecy.*

Degree levels of Freemasonry also have crowns. It revels in its deception. In this crown, there is a fantasy that cooperates with harlotry. Simply look at the titles of the various degrees of freemasonry. It's almost as if they created a weird world with fantastical titles. This is the defilement of the imagination.

This crown not only seeks silence but also mocks the sons. Its mouth is full of corruption, indignity, and falsehood. It's stealthy.

Every secret will be revealed. Secrets shroud, but the uncovering is unbearable. It is the Lord who uncovers that many times.

This head of the dragon seeks
to shame and silence the sons.
Have no secrets within you.

Recently, the pastor of a large church in the southwest of the United States was forced to resign due to something that happened with an underage woman many years ago. His secret came out, silencing and shaming him.

The old saying, "Be sure your sin will find you out, has much truth in it."

Remove and destroy
this crown from your head.
It is unbecoming of a son.

James 5:16:

> ***Confess your trespasses to one another****, and pray for one another, that you may be healed. The effective, fervent prayer of a righteous man avails much. (Emphasis mine)*

Regret is in this crown. You must crush this serpent under your feet.

Don't fall into its trap. *Govern* this crown, remove it, and destroy it. The sons bear the responsibility of secrets.

Deuteronomy 29:29:

> *The secret things belong to the LORD our God, but those things which are revealed belong to us and to our children forever, that we may do all the words of this law. (Emphasis mine)*

Psalms 25:14:

> *The secret of the LORD is with those who fear Him, and He will show them His covenant.*

Mark 4:22:

> *For there **is nothing that is hidden that won't be disclosed**, and **there is no secret that won't be brought out into the light!** (Emphasis mine)*

Personal Court Case
for the Removal of the Crown of Secrets

Father, I ask to step into Your Court of Mercy, through Jesus, on behalf of me and my generations. I ask that the accuser of the brethren be brought in as well as our generational line, from both sides of the family, and those who are with us by blood, marriage, adoption, civil or religious covenant, from your hand in the garden and all the way forward as far as it needs to go, as well as my cloud of witnesses.

I want to repent for myself and my generation, who kept secrets and took this crown willingly. I reveled in harlotry, took on shame, co-labored with deception, allowed it to mock, and caused our silencing of Your voice. As a governing son, forgive us and our generations for the secrets and for even having secrets about other people and using those secrets against them.

I repent for not taking this crown off our own heads, not confessing our sins one to another so that we could be healed, and not confessing these things to you. We harbored them in our hearts and acted like you didn't know. I repent for where we acted as if you couldn't see, and where we kept a secret. And we even smiled about it and reveled in it.

Forgive us and our generations, and forgive us where we took the throne and the seat of Freemasonry within our generations and did not present the throne and the crown to you.

I take it, and I crush it—this inferior crown under our feet—the head of the snake, the head of this dragon, I crush it and present to you the throne and request that the angels utterly destroy it, and the altar, and the idols of secrecy be judged in Your court this day as I repent on behalf of the generations for they did not know what they were doing. I ask that a complete capture of every demonic spirit that was used be made. Forgive us where your voice through us was silenced.

Because of this, I ask that angels crush shame and regret, and I ask for the amendment of 'As if it Never Were' as your blood pours through our generations, that the angels would go and remove every Crown of Secrets in the bloodline and destroy it.

Forgive us when we uncover secrets about others and bring them shame due to the knowledge we possess. I accept, Father, the scripture that everything done in secret is brought to light—your light. I ask this in the name of Jesus.

I thank You, Father, I thank You, Jesus, and I thank you, John, for your transparency as we learn that transparency is godly—no secrets.

I repent for any cooperation with Baal in any form at any time. I turn our back to the altar of Baal and ask angels to destroy every altar of Baal. I ask for a divorce from Baal, Lucifer, the red dragon, the Book of Magic, and any ungodly attraction. I ask that all debris associated with this cooperation with Baal be removed and destroyed on our behalf. I remove the regalia associated with this ungodly marriage covenant and request to be clothed in robes of righteousness.

I request that the head of this snake be cut off from the other heads and this dragon.

I ask that you please destroy and burn this inferior crown set on the seven-headed dragon, the dragon, its seven heads, its inferior crowns, thrones, mantles, scepters, altars, spiritual residue, essences, and debris, in Jesus' name.

I ask that the Superior Crowns of the Kingdom of Heaven be placed upon our heads, overturning the enormity of our sins.

I ask for renewed authorization for every crown restored to us, and those to be restored today in Your court, as well as the release of every mantle, throne, scepter, altar, anointing, Glory, and resources., and Glory.

I ask for Your righteous verdict or further counsel.

> [If further counsel is advised, follow these instructions. Once you have received a righteous verdict, begin the following segment:]

I speak to the earth that every one of our generations who stepped upon you, even those related to us by blood, marriage, adoption, civil or religious covenant.

Earth, I have received a righteous verdict from the Courts of Heaven this day. I bless you to hear the word of the Lord. I bless you to swallow up the iniquity and the egregious sins of self-deception and wearing these inferior crowns. Swallow up every word and deed that was done upon you. Swallow the innocent bloodshed, sexual sins, moving of the boundary stones, worship of ourselves, idol worship, occultic worship, theft...every sin under the sun that Jesus died for. I charge you to swallow it up and bless you to your original design. I bless you to see the governing sons and to begin blessing us. Begin pouring out your riches of abundance of truth and life.

I request the blood of Jesus to cover every place this was done upon you or in you. I speak to the frequencies of the wind to blow away the evil, to the water to drown it, and to the fire to burn it. I speak to you to return to your original design as the Lord had created you. The Earth is the Lord's, and its fullness belongs to the Lord.

I speak peace. I thank the Just Judge. I thank You, Jesus, the author and the finisher of our faith, for the Crowns of Righteousness and the Crown of Love that trump this inferior crown.

As a governing son, I pick up these Superior Crowns, place them upon our heads, and ask you to help us rule. I commission the angels to render these righteous verdicts in the spirit and the natural. I commission the angels to put this on record.

Thank you, Just Judge, for honoring us and trusting us with the responsibility of wearing these Crowns of Love and Righteousness. Thank you for helping us occupy the territory you assigned us. I don't take this lightly and ask for supernatural assistance and help daily to govern well as Your sons, in the name of Jesus.

As a son, I call in the treasure lost from the north, the south, the east, and the west in every age, realm, dimension, and time to fill the capacity of this section.

I ask that all of this be done in time and out of time, and in every age, realm, and dimension, and that all of the spiritual debris, residue, and essences that were left behind by this inferior crown and the spirits that came with it be destroyed utterly. Thank You, Father, for what you did. Thank you, Jesus, for giving us authority and dominion here.

Court Case
for Removal of the Crown of Secrets
Off of Someone

Father, I ask to step into Your Court of Mercy on behalf of _____ through Jesus, on behalf of them and their generations.

I ask that the accuser of the brethren be brought in as well as our generational line, from both sides of the family, and those who are with us by blood, marriage, adoption, civil or religious covenant, from your hand in the garden and all the way forward as far as it needs to go, as well as my cloud of witnesses.

I want to repent on behalf of them and their generations, who kept secrets and took this crown willingly. They reveled in harlotry, took on shame, co-labored with deception, allowed it to mock, and caused the silencing of Your voice. As governing sons, forgive them and their generations for their secrets and for having secrets about others, and for using those secrets against them.

I repent on their behalf for them not taking this crown off their own heads, not confessing their sins one to another so that they could be healed, not confessing these things to you. They harbored them in their hearts and acted like you didn't know. I repent where they acted like you couldn't see, and where they kept secrets. And they even smiled about it and reveled in it.

Forgive them and their generations, and forgive them where they took the throne and the seat of Freemasonry within their generations and did not present the throne and the crown to you.

As a governing son, I take it and I crush this inferior crown under their feet—I crush the head of this dragon and present to you the throne and request that the angels utterly destroy it, the altar(s), and the idols of secrecy. May they be judged in Your court this day as I repent on behalf of them and their generations, for they did not really know what they were doing. I ask for a complete capture of every demonic spirit that was used be made. Forgive us where your voice through them was silenced.

Because of this, I ask that angels crush shame and regret, and I ask for the amendment of 'As if it Never Were' as your blood pours through their generations, that the angels would go and remove every Crown of Secrets in the bloodline and destroy it.

Forgive them when they expose others and bring them shame because of the secret they knew. Father, I accept the scripture that everything done in secret is brought to light—your light. I ask this in the name of Jesus.

I repent for cooperation with Baal in any form at any time. I turn our back to the altar of Baal and ask angels to destroy every altar of Baal. I ask for a divorce from Baal, Lucifer, the red dragon, the Book of Magic, and any ungodly attraction. I ask that all debris associated with this cooperation with Baal be removed and destroyed on their behalf. I remove the regalia associated with this ungodly marriage covenant and request to be clothed in robes of righteousness.

I request that the head of this snake be cut off from the other heads and this dragon.

I ask that you please destroy and burn this inferior crown set on the seven-headed dragon, the dragon, its seven heads, its inferior crowns, thrones, mantles, scepters, altars, spiritual residue, essences, and debris, in Jesus' name.

I ask for the Superior Crowns of the Kingdom of Heaven to be placed on our heads, overturning the egregiousness of our sins.

I ask for renewed authorization for every crown restored to us, and those to be restored today in Your court, as well as the release of every mantle, throne, dominion, scepter, altar, anointing, Glory, and resources.

I ask for Your righteous verdict or further counsel.

> [If further counsel is advised, follow these instructions. Once you have received a righteous verdict, begin the following segment:]

I speak to the earth that every one of their generations who stepped upon you, even those related to them by blood, marriage, adoption, civil or religious covenant.

Earth, I have received a righteous verdict from the Courts of Heaven this day. I bless you to hear the word of the Lord. I bless you to swallow up the iniquity and the egregious sins of self-deception and wearing these inferior crowns. Swallow up every word and deed that was done upon you. Swallow the innocent bloodshed, sexual sins, moving of the boundary stones, worship of ourselves, idol worship, occultic worship, theft...every sin under the sun that Jesus died for. I charge you to swallow it up and bless you to your original design. I bless you to see the governing sons and to begin blessing them. Begin pouring out your riches of abundance of truth and life.

I request the blood of Jesus to cover every place this was done upon you or in you. I speak to the frequencies of the wind to blow away the evil, to the water to drown it, and to the fire to burn it. I speak to you to return to your original design as the Lord had created you. The Earth is the Lord's, and its fullness belongs to the Lord.

I speak peace to you. I thank the Just Judge. I thank You, Jesus, the author and the finisher of our faith, for the Crowns of Righteousness and the Crown of Love that trump this inferior crown.

As a governing son, I pick up these Superior Crowns, place them upon their heads, and ask you to help them rule. I commission the angels to render these righteous verdicts in the spirit and the natural. I commission the angels to put this on record.

Thank you, Just Judge, for honoring us and trusting us with the responsibility of wearing these Crowns of Love and Righteousness. Thank you for helping us occupy the territory you assigned us. I don't take this lightly and ask for supernatural assistance and help daily to govern well as Your sons, in the name of Jesus.

As a son, I call in the treasure lost to them and their generations from the north, the south, the east, and the west in every age, realm, dimension, and time to fill the capacity of this section.

I ask that all of this be done in time and out of time, and in every age, realm, and dimension, and that all of the spiritual debris, residue, and essences that were left behind by this inferior crown and the spirits that came with it be destroyed utterly. I thank You, Father, for what you did, Jesus, for giving us authority and dominion here.

However, Mark 4:22 says:

> *For there **is nothing that is hidden that won't be disclosed,** and **there is no secret that won't be brought out into the light!** (Emphasis mine)*

We knew we had one more crown to learn about, but a summary of its characteristics is in order.

Instructions to the Sons:

- Remove and destroy this crown from your head. It is unbecoming of a son.
- Repent for any involvement with this crown at any time, fashion, or place.
- You are to govern, remove, and destroy this crown.
- Crush this serpent under your feet.

Characteristics of the Crown of Secrets

- It seeks to silence the sons.
- It mocks the sons.
- It seeks to shame the sons
- It is bloodthirsty.
- Its screams of desire pierce frequencies.
- It walks with the spirit of death.

- Its inner workings are harlotry, divination, and mockery.
- Intercession of the sons excoriates the head of the dragon.
- Pharisees wore this crown.
- Violence comes from the mouth of this dragon to those who wear this crown.
- It covers itself with a cloak.
- It is the seat of Freemasonry that has a throne.
- It is shrouded.
- It revels in its deception.
- It is involved in the defilement of the imagination.
- Its mouth is full of corruption, indignity, and falsehood.
- It is stealthy in nature.
- Its secrets are nothing but lies.
- There is no truth in it.
- Regret is in this crown.
- It is the primary crown of Freemasonry.

Identifying the False Crown of Secrets

- Do they appear religious on the surface?
- Do they mock believers?
- Do they seek to silence believers?
- Do they shame people?
- Do they "kick back" at the thought of intercession?
- Are they violent when challenged?

- Are they involved in Freemasonry or other secret organizations?
- Will they disparage someone of a different mindset?
- Do they appear religious on the surface?

———— ∞ ————

Chapter 13

The False Crown of Antichrist

This crown is full of pomp and circumstance. There is an *elitism* to those who wear this crown. They have a 'Better than you' attitude." It looks down on people.

It has an air of superiority and a superiority complex, not unlike the Sadducees and teachers of the Law in the New Testament. This is the crown that the antichrist will wear.

Those who wear this crown *are indoctrinated*. The ones with this crown have multiple purposes. This crown works with the Crown of Secrets, and it also works with the Crown of Deceit. The ones who wear this crown can easily put on the Crown of Deception. This crown is noteworthy.

This crown clings to the cross but in defilement. It is superstitious, seeks fame, is pretentious, full of pride, lofty, arrogant, and judges. This crown *has infiltrated the church*. This crown calls in the Delilah's, the Jezebel's, and the Ahab's. It has the deadliest bite. In its bite, there are many poisons. This crown *has led more astray* than any of the other crowns. That's what makes it noteworthy. This is the Crown of Antichrist. It embodies false religion. It has a realm.

---

*It is the Crown of Antichrist,
there is a Realm of Antichrist
and a Spirit of Antichrist
as well as an Office of Antichrist.*

Many would believe that the unsaved wear this crown, but it is upon those in the church, those with the deadly bite, and those who co-conspire with the spirit, the office, and the realm of the antichrist.

It has polluted the church, the Body of Christ, and the ecclesia. Those who are bitten by those who wear this crown often leave the Body of Christ and never return. Over the last several years, you have probably heard or been aware of pastors who have suddenly announced they no longer believe in God. They have taken this crown.

---

*Its main goal and focus
are to bring an end to the
embodiment of the church.*

> *To deal with it, remove not only its mantle, the crown, and its seat, which is a throne, but also the Delilah's.*

Focus on the repentance work and on the work of those in the body of Christ who have been elevated to positions and seats of power. To those who have ruling and rank over the people, and to those who have tolerated Jezebel.[8] But also *close the portal, remove its garments*, and *request that the head of this snake be cut off from the rest*. It empowers and emboldens those whose lust *is* power and greed, and it enslaves those under it.

> *You must break off the chains of enslavement from this crown for the people.*

It may appear harmless on the surface, but its bite is deadly and poisonous.

One of the ways it operates in conjunction with the Crown of Secrets is through the infiltration of Freemasonry and the Eastern Star within the church.

---

[8] See Revelation 2:20–toleration of Jezebel implies toleration of sexual sin in essentially any form, self-gratification, pornography, fornication, adultery, incest, homosexuality, bestiality, etc.

Many spiritual leaders, pastors, and clergy are Freemasons or are involved in the Eastern Star. This crown will reach over and place the Crown of Deceit or Deception on people's heads.

This crown has an office, too — the Office of the Crown of Antichrist. This crown is specifically designed to work in conjunction with the Crown of Secrets and the Crown of Deceit or Deception. It will cause you to be delusional, have delusions of grandeur, and be secretive. How many pastors and how many churches have been covered in secrets?"

It's not just about removing this crown; you must *remove its mantle, destroy the seat,* and *close the portal.* You must *break the chains from those who have been impacted or who have agreed with one who wears this crown* and *those who were over you."*

Steps to Freedom from the Crown of Antichrist.

To remove this crown, you must:

1. Remove its mantle.
2. Destroy the seat.
3. Close the portal.
4. Break the chains.

Personal Court Case
for the Removal of the Crown of Antichrist

Father, I ask to step into the Mercy Court of Heaven to receive Mercy in our time of need. I request the accuser of the brethren be brought in as well as my entire generations and everyone related to me by blood, marriage, adoption, civil or religious covenant, from Your hand in the garden, and all the way forward as far as it needs to go, as well as my cloud of witnesses.

Your Honor, I agree with the adversary that my generation bowed our knees to this dragon, accepted the inferior crowns, and wore them proudly. I repent for the spirit of antichrist we bore and the inferior crown we took upon our heads. I repent for the pomp and circumstance, elitism, better-than-you attitude, superiority complex, and indoctrination we took on, as well as the indoctrination of others; I repent for embodying a false religion and for 'biting' those we were in stewardship over, releasing the poison. I repent for working with the false Crown of Delusion and the false Crown of Secrets. I repent for all the secrets this inferior crown bore that we agreed with.

I repent for conspiring with the office, realm, and spirit of antichrist, for embodying it. I repent for participating in exploiting, polluting, and poisoning the church, the body, and the ecclesia. I repent for being a part of an end to bodies of Ecclesias, people, and churches. I repent for allowing, tolerating, being in league with, and cooperating with the Delilah spirit, Jezebel, and Ahab. I repent for opening up an evil portal and creating evil timelines for us, our generations, and others. I repent for taking on this mantle, sitting on the seat/office/throne, and ruling unjustly over your people. I repent for seeking to be elevated to positions and seats of power or where we, who wore this inferior crown, elevated those who should not ever have been elevated. I repent for the pride and for lusting after power and greed.

I repent for the false clinging to the cross, the defilement and mockery of it, for seeking fame, being pretentious, full of pride, lofty, arrogant, and judging others. I repent for embodying false religion, for promoting and esteeming it. Forgive us and our generations for infiltrating the church, bringing this inferior crown and elevating others to it. Forgive us for leading others astray.

I request your blood, Jesus, the amendment of 'As If It Never Were,' the destruction of the seat/office/throne, the closing of the portal, and the removal of the garments. Please remove its mantle, destroy the seat, and close the portal. I ask that you break the chains from those who have been impacted or who have agreed with those who have worn this inferior crown over the generations, and those we were over. Please have these destroyed.

I request that the chains attached to us and our generations be cut, severed, destroyed, and dismantled, and the ashes of them be brought to Jesus. I request a complete destruction, annulment, cancellation, and overturning of the office of the Crown of Antichrist, in the name of Jesus.

I also request that the angels clean up the spiritual debris, essences, and residues in time, out of time, and in every age, realm, and dimension to infinity. Burn it and give the ashes to Jesus.

I ask that you please destroy and burn this inferior crown set on the seven-headed dragon, the dragon, its seven heads, its inferior crowns, thrones, mantles, scepters, altars, spiritual residue, essences, and debris, in Jesus' name.

I ask for the Superior Crowns of the Kingdom of Heaven to be placed on our heads, overturning the egregiousness of our sins.

I ask for renewed authorization for every crown restored to us, and those to be restored today in Your court and the release of every mantle, throne, scepter, altar, anointing, Glory, and resources., and Glory.

I ask for Your righteous verdict or further counsel.

> [If further repentance is needed, follow the instructions of the court.]

With our righteous verdict in hand, I speak to the Earth. I speak to you that every one of our generations who stepped upon you, even those related to us by blood, marriage, adoption, civil or religious covenant. Earth, I have received a righteous verdict from the Courts of Heaven this day.

I bless you to hear the word of the Lord. I bless you to swallow up the iniquity and the egregious sins of wearing these inferior crowns. Swallow up every word and deed that was done upon you. Swallow the innocent bloodshed, sexual sins, moving of the boundary stones, worship of ourselves, idol worship, occultic worship, theft...every sin under the sun that Jesus died for.

I charge you to swallow it up, and I bless you to your original design; I bless you to see the governing sons and to begin blessing us. Begin pouring out your riches of the abundance of the truth of life. I request the blood of Jesus to cover every place this was done upon you, in you. I speak to the frequencies of the wind to blow away the evil. To the water, to drown it, and to the fire to burn it. I speak to you to return to your original design as the Lord had created you, the earth. The earth is the Lord's, and its fullness belongs to the Lord.

I speak peace, and I thank You, Jesus. I thank the Just Judge. I thank You, Jesus, the author and the finisher of our faith. I commission the angels to render these righteous verdicts in the spirit and the natural.

I commission the angels to put this on record. Thank you, Just Judge, for honoring us and trusting us with the responsibility of wearing the Crown of Love and the Crown of Righteousness. Thank you for helping us occupy the territory you assigned us. I don't take this lightly and ask for supernatural assistance and help daily to govern well as Your sons, in the name of Jesus.

As a son, I call in the treasure lost from the north, the south, the east, and the west in every age, realm, dimension, and time to fill the capacity of this section.

I am grateful to Heaven for revealing the red dragon, its inferior crowns, and its mission. I am grateful that Revelation tells us that God himself has pierced this dragon. Thank you for your kindness in helping us overcome the word of our testimony and the blood of the lamb.

I ask that all of this be done in time and out of time, and in every age, realm, and dimension, and that all of the spiritual debris, residue, and essences that were left behind by this inferior crown and the spirits that came with it be destroyed utterly. I thank You, Father, for what you did, Jesus, for giving us authority and dominion here.

Court Case
for the Removal of the Crown of Antichrist
Off of Someone

Father, I ask to step into the Mercy Court of Heaven on behalf of _____ to receive Mercy in our time of need. I request the accuser of the brethren be brought in as well as them and their entire generations and everyone related to them by blood, marriage, adoption, civil or religious covenant, from Your hand in the garden, and all the way forward as far as it needs to go, as well as my cloud of witnesses.

Your Honor, I agree with the adversary that they and their generations bowed their knees to this dragon, accepted the inferior crowns, and wore them proudly. I repent for the spirit of antichrist they bore and the inferior crown they took upon their heads. I repent for the pomp and circumstance, elitism, indoctrination, better-than-you attitude, and superiority complex we took on, as well as the indoctrination of others; I repent for embodying a false religion and for 'biting' those they were in stewardship over, releasing the poison. I repent for working with the false Crown of Delusion as well as the false Crown of Secrets. I repent for all of the secrets this inferior crown bore that they agreed with.

I repent for conspiring with the office, realm, and spirit of antichrist, for embodying it. I repent for participating in exploiting, polluting, and poisoning the church, the body, and the ecclesia. I repent for being a part of an end to bodies of Ecclesias, people, and churches. I repent for allowing, tolerating, being in league with, and cooperating with the Delilah spirit, Jezebel, and Ahab. We repent for opening up an evil portal and creating evil timelines for us, our generations, and others. We repent for taking on this mantle, sitting on the seat, the throne, and in the office of antichrist and ruling unjustly over your people. I repent for seeking to be elevated to positions and seats of power or where they, who wore this inferior crown, elevated those who should not ever have been elevated. I repent for the pride and for lusting after power and greed.

I repent for the false clinging to the cross, the defilement and mockery of it, for seeking fame, being pretentious, full of pride, lofty, arrogant, and judging others. I repent for embodying false religion, for promoting and esteeming it. Forgive us and our generations for infiltrating the church, bringing this inferior crown and elevating others to it. Forgive us for leading others astray.

I request your blood, Jesus, the amendment of 'As If It Never Were', the destruction of the seat/office/throne, the closing of the portal, and the removal of the garments. Please remove its mantle, destroy the seat, and close the portal. I ask that you break the chains from those who have been impacted or who have agreed with those who have worn this inferior crown over the generations and those whom they were over. Please have these destroyed.

I request that the chains attached to us and our generations be cut, severed, destroyed, and dismantled, and the ashes of them be brought to Jesus. I request a full destruction, annulment, cancellation, and overturning of the office of the Crown of Antichrist, in the name of Jesus.

I also request that the angels clean up the spiritual debris, essences, and residues in time, out of time, and in every age, realm, and dimension to infinity. Burn it and give the ashes to Jesus.

I ask for Your righteous verdict or further counsel.

[If further repentance is needed, follow the instructions of the court.]

With our righteous verdict in hand, I speak to the Earth. I speak to you that every one of our generations who stepped upon you, even those related to us by blood, marriage, adoption, civil or religious covenant. Earth, I have received a righteous verdict from the Courts of Heaven this day.

I bless you to hear the word of the Lord. I bless you to swallow up the iniquity and the egregious sins of wearing these inferior crowns. Swallow up every word and deed that was done upon you. Swallow the innocent bloodshed, sexual sins, moving of the boundary stones, worship of ourselves, idol worship, occultic worship, theft...every sin under the sun that Jesus died for.

I charge you to swallow it up, and I bless you to your original design; I bless you to see the governing sons and to begin blessing us. Begin pouring out your riches of the abundance of the truth of life. I request the blood of Jesus to cover every place this was done upon you, in you. I speak to the frequencies of the wind to blow away the evil. To the water, to drown it, and to the fire to burn it. I speak to you to come back to your original design as the Lord had created you, the earth. The earth is the Lord's, and its fullness belongs to the Lord.

I speak peace, and I thank You, Jesus. I thank the Just Judge. I thank You, Jesus, the author and the finisher of our faith. I commission the angels to render these righteous verdicts in the spirit and the natural.

I commission the angels to put this on record. Thank you, Just Judge, for honoring us and trusting us with the responsibility of wearing the Crown of Love and the Crown of Righteousness. Thank you for helping us occupy the territory you assigned us. I don't take this lightly and ask for supernatural assistance and help daily to govern well as Your sons, in the name of Jesus.

As a son, I call in the treasure lost from the north, the south, the east, and the west in every age, realm, dimension, and time to fill the capacity of this section.

I are grateful to Heaven for revealing the red dragon, its inferior crowns, and its mission. I am grateful that Revelation tells us that God has pierced this dragon. Thank you for your kindness in helping us overcome the word of our testimony and the blood of the lamb.

I ask that all of this be done in time and out of time, and in every age, realm, and dimension, and that all of the spiritual debris, residue, and essences that were left behind by this inferior crown and the spirits that came with it be destroyed utterly. Thank You, Father, for what you did. Thank you, Jesus, for giving us authority and dominion here.

Characteristics of the False Crown of Antichrist

- This crown is full of pomp and circumstance.

- There's an elitism to those who wear this crown, a 'Better than you' attitude."
- It has an air of superiority and a superiority complex.
- Those who wear this crown are indoctrinated.
- The ones with this crown have multiple purposes.
- It works with the Crown of Secrets and the Crown of Deception.
- Those who wear this crown can easily wear the Crown of Deception.
- This crown is noteworthy.
- This crown clings to the cross but in defilement.
- It is superstitious.
- It seeks fame.
- It is pretentious. It is full of pride
- It is lofty.
- It is arrogant.
- It judges.
- This crown has the deadliest bite. In its bite, there are many poisons.
- This crown has infiltrated the church.
- This crown calls in the Delilahs, the Jezebels, and the Ahabs.
- This crown has led more astray than any of the other crowns.
- It embodies false religion.
- It has a realm.
- It empowers.

- It emboldens those whose lust is power and greed.
- It enslaves those under it.
- It is embodied in those in the church.
- It has polluted the church, the Body of Christ, and the Ecclesia.
- Those who are bitten by those who wear this crown often leave the Body of Christ and never return.
- Its main goal and focus are to bring an end to the embodiment of the body, which is the church.

Solutions

- Remove not only its mantle, the crown, and its seat, which is a throne, but also the Delilah's.
- Focus on the repentance work of those in the body of Christ who have been elevated to positions and seats of power. To those who have rule and rank over the people, and to those who have tolerated Jezebel.
- Close the portal.
- Remove its garments.
- Request that the head of this snake be cut off from the rest.
- You must break off the chains of enslavement from this crown for the people.

Identifying the False Crown of Antichrist

- Are they full of pomp and circumstance?
- Do they exhibit a "better-than-thou" attitude?
- Do they have an air of elitism?
- Do they have a superiority complex?
- Are they indoctrinated?
- Are they religious outwardly, but it doesn't seem real?
- Are they superstitious?
- Do they seek fame?
- Are they pretentious?
- Are they full of pride?
- Are they arrogant?
- Are they lofty?
- Are they judgmental?
- Are they in league with Jezebel, Delilah, or Ahab?
- Do they have a lust for power?
- Do they enslave those who are beneath them?
- Do they express the thought that Jesus can't handle certain situations or that Jesus isn't enough?

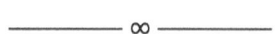

Chapter 14

The False Crown of Devouring

The seventh false crown is the *Crown of Devouring*. This head of the dragon is seeking whomever he may devour. He sniffs out the weak, sniffs out those on the edge, and he seeks whom he can devour. The dragon hunts after the sons to place this crown upon them. This is a fierce crown in league with the sons of perdition—the ones that have given themselves over to darkness, also referred to as Sons of Belial or S.O.B's.

Because sin leaves a stench, the dragon hunts you. He follows the trail of the stench of sin. If sin is in your life, he can smell you.

Jude 1:17-23:

> *17 But you, beloved, remember the words which were spoken before by the apostles of our Lord Jesus Christ: 18 how they told you that there would be mockers in the last time who would*

walk according to their own ungodly lusts. ¹⁹ These are sensual persons, who cause divisions, not having the Spirit.

²⁰ But you, beloved, building yourselves up on your most holy faith, praying in the Holy Spirit, ²¹ keep yourselves in the love of God, looking for the mercy of our Lord Jesus Christ unto eternal life. ²² And on some have compassion, making a distinction; ²³ but others save with fear, pulling them out of the fire, **hating even the garment defiled by the flesh.** *(Emphasis mine)*

Some follow *darkness,* while others fall into it. There is a difference. This dragon hunts both. Most don't return when this crown is put upon their head. It's lethal. That's what devouring does.

With this crown, you lose all sensibility and sense of oneness.

The most hardened of hearts wear this crown.

This isn't just an atheistic view; this is <u>a hatred of God</u>, a turning away, and the true son of perdition. It's not like the average sinner wears this crown. This dragon *seeks to devour common sense* and commonalities in people's lives so they cannot hear the voice of God or see God. That is what this dragon seeks—to devour the truth. The darkest of the dark wear this crown.

To watch the news, you probably have said, "They have lost their minds!" That is what this devouring crown does. You lose all sense of reason. If you encounter someone with whom you cannot reason and who appears to lack common sense, this individual is likely under the influence of this crown.

It's not the average atheist or sinner who wears this crown. This is like the deepest, darkest, blackest-hearted people. The ones that consume babies and murder and are on a path of what we would call the evil ones. An example would be Adolf Hitler or some of his assistants. It is sniffing out sin. It works in tandem with all other crowns because it seeks to devour.

2 Thessalonians 2:3:

> *Let no one deceive you by any means; for that day will not come unless the falling away comes first, and the man of sin is revealed, the* **son of perdition**. *(Emphasis mine)*

John 17:12:

> *While I was with them in the world, I kept them in Your name. Those whom You gave Me I have kept; and none of them is lost except* **the son of perdition**, *that the Scripture might be fulfilled. (Emphasis mine)*

> *There is no light in them.*
> *There is only darkness.*

Perdition typically refers to the state of perishing, being lost, dying, or being destroyed.

They have no light in them. These are the ones that he is seeking whom he can devour and take to hell with him. When you sin, it begins sniffing you out.

He is roaming about and seeking to devour things. He has been looking for the crowns. The roaming is about seeking those whose crown he can claim. The other crowns must be removed before addressing this one.

Atheists and those family members who don't believe they are wearing this crown, but they have purposefully stepped over into something dark. *They have no conscience.*

Personal Court Case for Removal of a Crown of Devouring

[Repentance for this crown needs to follow repentance for all the other crowns.]

Father, I ask to step into Your Court of Mercy to receive mercy in our time of need. I ask that the accuser of the brethren be brought into this court as well as my generations, those related to me by blood, marriage, civil and religious covenant, all the way back to Your hand in the garden and all the way forward as far as it needs to go, and my cloud of witnesses.

Your Honor, this Crown of Devouring cannot be removed until the other crowns are removed. However, I would like to begin the court case process today.

Your Honor, I repent for myself and my generations for partnering, agreeing with, and participating with the darkest of the darkest of sins. I repent that I put myself and our generations in danger of being hunted because of these sins. I repent for our weaknesses in not seeking after God. I repent for our generations' sins that created a stench that the enemy could sniff out.

I repent for living on the edge, allowing this dragon to hunt us and those in our generations. I repent for being in league with the sons of perdition—the ones that have given themselves over to darkness. I repent for losing all sensibility and sense of oneness of our spirit, soul, and body in cooperation with the Lord. I repent for becoming and having the most hardened of hearts. I repent for having deliberately stepped into something dark and for agreeing to have no conscience.

I repent for allowing ourselves to be void of truth. I repent for taking up the other crowns and then wearing this one, the last. I repent for the lust of blood, the drinking of blood, and the eating of flesh from the kingdom of darkness. We are only to take in the blood and body of Christ. I repent for ourselves and our generations. I repent for the idea of getting near the unholy fire and letting it burn us and for basking in it, allowing it to consume us.

I request that all crowns be destroyed and that this specific crown be fully removed and destroyed, as I have done the repentance work. I request the full removal of this vile crown from our heads as well as from the heads of our generations. I ask that it be burned in the Holy Fire of the Lord God Almighty.

I request the amendment of 'As if it Never Were' and ask for restoration in the mighty name of Jesus.

Please burn the spiritual residue, essences, and debris. In Jesus' name, I ask for the Superior Crowns of the Kingdom of Heaven to be placed on our heads, overturning the egregiousness of our sins.

I ask for Your righteous verdict, your honor or further counsel.

> [If further counsel is advised, follow these instructions. Once you have received a righteous verdict, begin the following segment:]

I speak to the earth that every one of our generations who stepped upon you, even those related to us by blood, marriage, adoption, civil or religious covenant.

Earth, I have received a righteous verdict from the Courts of Heaven this day. I bless you to hear the word of the Lord. I bless you to swallow up the iniquity and the egregious sins of self-deception and wearing these crowns. Swallow up every word and deed that was done upon you. Swallow the innocent bloodshed, sexual sins, moving of the boundary stones, worship of ourselves, idol worship, occultic worship, theft...every sin under the sun that Jesus died for. I charge you to swallow it up and bless you to your original design. I bless you to see the governing sons and to begin blessing us. Begin pouring out your riches of abundance of truth and life.

I request the blood of Jesus to cover every place this was done upon you or in you. I speak to the frequencies of the wind to blow away the evil, to the water to drown it, and to the fire to burn it. I speak to you to return to your original design as the Lord had created you. The Earth is the Lord's, and its fullness belongs to the Lord.

I speak peace. I thank the Just Judge. I thank You, Jesus, the author and the finisher of our faith, for the Crowns of Righteousness and the Crown of Love that trump this inferior crown.

As a governing son, I pick up these Superior Crowns, place them upon our heads, and ask you to help us rule. I commission the angels to render these righteous verdicts in the spirit and the natural. I commission the angels to put this on record.

Thank you, Just Judge, for honoring us and trusting us with the responsibility of wearing these Crowns of Love and Righteousness. Thank you for helping us occupy the territory you assigned us. I don't take this lightly and ask for supernatural assistance and help daily to govern well as Your sons, in the name of Jesus.

> As a son, I call in the treasure lost from the north, the south, the east, and the west in every age, realm, dimension, and time to fill the capacity of this section.

> I ask that all of this be done in time and out of time, and in every age, realm, and dimension, and that all of the spiritual debris, residue, and essences that were left behind by this inferior crown and the spirits that came with it be destroyed utterly. I thank You, Father, for what you did, Jesus, for giving us authority and dominion here.

Court Case
for Removal of a Crown of Devouring
Off of Someone

[Repentance for this crown needs to follow repentance for all the other crowns.]

Father, I ask to step into Your Court of Mercy on behalf of _____ to receive mercy in time of need. I ask that the accuser of the brethren be brought into this court as well as their generations, those related to them by blood, marriage, civil and religious covenant, all the way back to Your hand in the garden and all the *way forward as far as it needs to go, and their cloud of witnesses.*

Your Honor, this false Crown of Devouring cannot be removed until the other false crowns are removed. However, I would like to begin the court case process today.

Your Honor, I repent for them and their generations for partnering, agreeing with, and participating with the darkest of the darkest of sins. I repent that they put themselves and their generations in danger of being hunted because of these sins. I repent for their weaknesses in not seeking after God. I repent for their generations' sins that created a stench that the enemy could sniff out.

I repent for them living on the edge, allowing this dragon to hunt them and those in their generations. I repent for them being in league with the sons of perdition—the ones that have given themselves over to darkness. I repent for them losing all sensibility and sense of oneness of our spirit, soul, and body in cooperation with the Lord. I repent for them becoming and having the most hardened of hearts. I repent for them having deliberately stepped into something dark and for agreeing to have no conscience.

I repent for allowing ourselves to be void of truth. I repent for them taking up the other crowns and then wearing this one. I repent for their lust of blood, for their drinking of blood, and the eating of flesh from the kingdom of darkness. We are only to take in the blood and body of Christ. I repent for them and their generations. I repent for the idea of getting near the unholy fire and letting it burn them and for basking in it, allowing it to consume them.

I request that all crowns be destroyed and that this specific crown be fully removed and destroyed, as I have done the repentance work. I request the full removal of this vile crown from our heads as well as from the heads of their generations. I ask that it be burned in the Holy Fire of the Lord God Almighty.

I request the amendment of 'As if it Never Were' and ask for restoration in the mighty name of Jesus.

Please burn the spiritual residue, essences, and debris. In Jesus' name, I ask for the Superior Crowns of the Kingdom of Heaven to be placed on their heads, overturning the egregiousness of their sins.

I ask for Your righteous verdict, Your Honor, or further counsel.

> [If further counsel is advised, follow these instructions. Once you have received a righteous verdict, begin the following segment:]

I speak to the earth that every one of their generations who stepped upon you, even those related to them by blood, marriage, adoption, civil or religious covenant.

Earth, I have received a righteous verdict from the Courts of Heaven this day. I bless you to hear the word of the Lord. I bless you to swallow up the iniquity and the egregious sins of self-deception and wearing these crowns. Swallow up every word and deed that was done upon you. Swallow the innocent bloodshed, sexual sins, moving of the boundary stones, worship of ourselves, idol worship, occultic worship, theft...every sin under the sun that Jesus died for. I charge you to swallow it up and bless you to your original design. I bless you to see the governing sons and to begin blessing us. Begin pouring out your riches of abundance of truth and life.

I request the blood of Jesus to cover every place this was done upon you or in you. I speak to the frequencies of the wind to blow away the evil, to the water to drown it, and to the fire to burn it. I speak to you to return to your original design as the Lord had created you. The Earth is the Lord's, and its fullness belongs to the Lord.

I speak peace. I thank the Just Judge. I thank You, Jesus, the author and the finisher of our faith, for the Crowns of Righteousness and the Crown of Love that trump this inferior crown.

As a governing son, I pick up these Superior Crowns, place them upon their heads, and ask you to help them rule. I commission the angels to render these righteous verdicts in the spirit and the natural. I commission the angels to put this on record.

Thank you, Just Judge, for honoring us and trusting us with the responsibility of wearing these Crowns of Love and Righteousness. Thank you for helping us occupy the territory you assigned us. I don't take this lightly and ask for supernatural assistance and help daily to govern well as Your sons, in the name of Jesus.

As a son, I call in the treasure lost to them and their generations from the north, the south, the east, and the west in every age, realm, dimension, and time to fill the capacity of this section.

I ask that all of this be done in time and out of time, in every age, realm, and dimension, and that all the spiritual debris, residue, and essences left behind by this inferior crown and the spirits accompanying it be utterly destroyed. Thank You, Father, for what you did. Thank you, Jesus, for giving us authority and dominion here.

Characteristics of the Crown of Devouring

- The head of this crown was seeking whom he may devour.
- He hunts after the sons.
- This is a fierce crown in league with the sons of perdition—the ones that have given themselves over to darkness.
- He follows the stench of sin.
- If you have sin in your life, he can smell you.

- There are those that follow darkness, and there are those that fall into darkness. There is a difference. This dragon hunts both.
- He has many crowns, and he seeks to devour.
- Most don't come back when they've had this crown put upon their head.
- It's lethal.
- With this crown, you lose all sensibility and sense of oneness.
- The most hardened of hearts wear this crown.
- Wearers of this crown have a hatred of God. They have turned away and are true sons of perdition.
- This dragon seeks to devour common sense and commonalities in people's lives.
- It devours truth.
- The darkest of the dark wear this crown.
- It works in tandem with all the other crowns because it's the one that seeks to devour.
- There is no light in them. There is only darkness.
- The other crowns must be removed before this crown is addressed.
- Those who wear this crown have stepped over into something really dark purposefully.
- They have no conscience.

Identifying the False Crown of Devouring

- Are they hiding secret sins?
- Are they heavily involved in darkness?

- Do their words express wickedness?
- Are they conniving?
- Do they have hardened hearts?
- Do they have sensibility?
- Do they have a sense of oneness?
- Do they have a hard heart?
- Do they seek to devour common sense?
- Do they seek to devour commonalities in people's lives?
- Do they despise the truth?
- Do they have no conscience?
- Are they filled with darkness?
- Have they stepped into a depth of darkness purposefully?

———— ∞ ————

Interaction of the Seven False Crowns

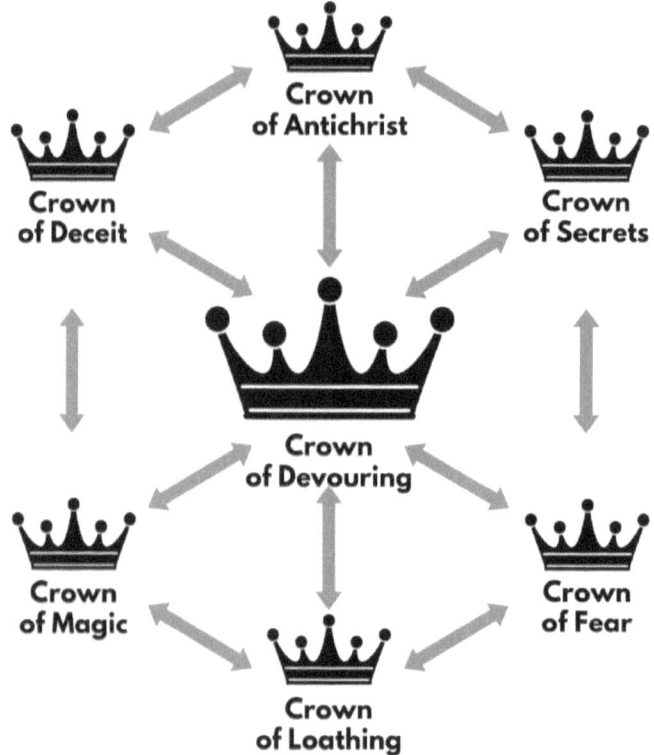

Chapter 15
Gaining Freedom
from the Seven False Crowns

If you have worked through the court case for freedom from all seven of the false crowns, you may want to wrap up the court work in this manner:

Personal Court Work
for Freedom from the Seven False Crowns

Father, I ask to step into Your Court of Crowns. I ask that the accuser of the brethren be brought into this court as well as my generations, those related to me by blood, marriage, civil and religious covenant, all the way back to Your hand in the garden and all the way forward as far as it needs to go.

I ask that the seven-headed dragon be brought in and muzzled and caged. I request that the accuser of the brethren and every Principality, power, demon, ruler of darkness, and evil entity that was associated with the seven-headed dragon, their inferior crowns, mantles, altars, thrones, and scepters, be brought in and gagged as well.

Having done repentance work for each of the seven crowns, Your Honor, I ask that the repentance work already accomplished and the verdicts be brought into evidence in this court this day. I also request our cloud of witnesses, the angels, and every witness to these events be brought into this court on our behalf.

I request that these seven heads be judged today, for they have inflicted pain, torment, anguish, and untold misery upon Your sons and daughters and the peoples of the earth. They have hindered the growth, abilities, expansion, and work of Your church on Earth. They have murdered, stolen, and destroyed without regard for You, Your sons, or Your purposes in the earth. They have laid evil and egregious crowns on the heads of Your sons to mock not only them but You.

I ask that each head be judged, cut off, and destroyed from our lives, and the damage be undone via the amendment of "As if it Never Were."

I ask that you please burn the inferior Crown of the Beast which is set above the seven-headed dragon, the dragon, its seven heads, its inferior crowns, thrones, mantles, scepters, altars, spiritual residue, essences, and debris. In Jesus' name, I ask for the Superior Crowns of the Kingdom of Heaven to be placed on our heads, overturning the egregiousness of our sins.

I ask for renewed authorization for every crown restored to us and those to be restored today in Your court.

I am grateful to Heaven for revealing the red dragon, its inferior crowns, associated evil entities, and its mission. I am grateful that Revelation tells us that this dragon has been pierced by God Himself. Thank You for your kindness in helping us overcome the word of our testimony and the blood of the lamb.

I ask that all of this be done in time and out of time, and in every age, realm, and dimension, and that all the spiritual debris, residue, and essences that were left behind by this inferior crown and the spirits that came with it be destroyed utterly. I also ask that these evil entities be judged in Your court this day, in Jesus' name.

I thank You, Father, for what you did, Jesus, for giving us the authority and dominion here.

Court Work for Freedom from the Seven False Crowns for Some Else

Father, I ask to step into Your Court of Crowns on behalf of _____. I ask that the accuser of the brethren be brought into this court as well as them and their generations, those related to us by blood, marriage, civil and religious covenant, all the way back to Your hand in the garden and all the way forward as far as it needs to go.

I ask that the seven-headed dragon be brought in and muzzled and caged. I request that the accuser of the brethren and every Principality, power, demon, ruler of darkness, and evil entity that was associated with the seven-headed dragon, their inferior crowns, mantles, altars, thrones, and scepters, be brought in and gagged as well.

Having done repentance work for each of the seven crowns, Your Honor, I ask that the repentance work already accomplished and the verdicts be brought into evidence in this court this day. I also request that they and their cloud of witnesses, the angels, and every witness to these events be brought into this court on their behalf.

I request that these seven heads be judged today, for they have inflicted pain, torment, anguish, and untold misery upon Your sons and daughters and the peoples of the earth. They have hindered the growth, abilities, expansion, and work of Your church on Earth. They have murdered, stolen, and destroyed without regard for You, Your sons, or Your purposes in the earth. They have laid evil and egregious crowns on the heads of Your sons to mock not only them but You.

I ask that each head be judged, cut off, and destroyed from our lives, and the damage be undone via the amendment of "As if it Never Were."

I ask that You please burn the inferior Crown of the Beast which is set above the seven-headed dragon, the dragon, its seven heads, its inferior crowns, thrones, mantles, scepters, altars, spiritual residue, essences, and debris. In Jesus' name, I ask for the Superior Crowns of the Kingdom of Heaven to be placed on our heads, overturning the egregiousness of our sins.

I ask for renewed authorization for every crown restored to us and those to be restored today in Your court.

I am grateful to Heaven for revealing the red dragon, its inferior crowns, associated evil entities, and its mission. I am grateful that Revelation tells us that this dragon has been pierced by God Himself. Thank You for Your kindness in helping us overcome the word of our testimony and the blood of the lamb.

I ask that all of this be done in time and out of time, in every age, realm, and dimension, and that all the spiritual debris, residue, and essences left behind by this inferior crown and the spirits that accompanied it be utterly destroyed. I also ask that these evil entities be judged in Your court this day, in the name of Jesus.

I thank You, Father, for what You did, Jesus, for giving us the authority and dominion here.

These seven false crowns are by no means the only ungodly crowns; they are simply seven primary categories of false crowns. These are the biggies. In your intercession, you will uncover and remove other ungodly crowns from these leaders, regardless of their title; the great news is that the Superior Crowns of Heaven always prevail.

———— ∞ ————

Chapter 16

Superior Crowns

Any crown from Heaven is superior to the inferior crowns that Satan has devised or corrupted. We want the Law of Exchange to work. We want the inferior false crowns that our leaders are wearing to be replaced with the Superior Crowns of Heaven.

Where you find an inferior Crown of Strife, you want it removed and replaced with a Superior Crown of the Shalom of God. Where you find an inferior crown of division, you want it removed, the works of the crown destroyed, and place a Crown of the Unity of Heaven in its stead.

Crowns are critical for the sons to understand. Authority in one's life can be reborn or reignited by the embrace of crowns. Some crowns come with a cost, while others are a result of the cost. The number of crowns available to the sons is immeasurable, for the

Father wants our authority to be immeasurable. We want to see every inferior crown bowing to a Superior Crown. The sick man in Acts at the temple gate was wearing a crown of sickness, and it needed to be exchanged for a Crown of Wholeness.

When people carry a Crown of Depression or defeat, that inferior crown must bow to the Superior Crown of Hope and Victory. When you see how many are bent low under the weight of an inferior crown, see that inferior crown bowing to a Superior Crown. That is how the will of Heaven manifests. Replace the inferior crowns with Superior Crowns.

Remember, the Word says that in the name of Jesus, every knee will bow, and every tongue will confess the Lordship of Jesus.[9] That is an inferior crown bowing to the Superior Crown.

The Authority of Inferior Crowns

A principle of the Word is that all crowns carry a degree of authority related to the type of crown they are. Therefore, if someone has received a Crown of Sickness, that crown will begin to manifest sickness of some sort in the person's body. As we learn to facilitate the exchange of inferior crowns with Superior Crowns, healing will manifest because a Crown of Wholeness

---

[9] Philippians 2:11

carries with it the authority to release wholeness into a person, thereby defeating the operation of the Crown of Sickness. Crowns are representative of the authority we carry in a particular arena.

> *Crowns are representative of the authority we carry in a particular arena.*

When you read authority-related verses, understand that the inferior is bowing to the superior. As the sons exercise the authority in the various crowns they carry, many who have been weighed down under the weight of inferior crowns will find those crowns coming off their heads and being replaced by the Superior Crown.

Every capability of the Father can be released and made resident in a crown. For healing, we have the expression of Jehovah Raphe (The Lord our Healer), for provision (Jehovah Jireh), for victory in battle, Jehovah Sabaoth (the Lord of Hosts), and more. His touch is in everything He has created. The crowns lack nothing.

> *You are responsible for the stewardship of the blessing contained in a particular crown.*

As you learn to walk and work from the authority of a Superior Crown, much will change. When you look in a mirror, see yourself carrying Superior Crowns.

In Luke 10:19, Jesus is speaking and says:

> *Look, I have given you authority (of a Superior Crown) over all the power (inferior crowns) of the enemy, and you can walk among snakes and scorpions (operations of inferior crowns) and crush them. Nothing will injure you. (NLT) (Emphasis mine)*

Have you noticed that when we lay hands on someone to pray for them, we generally lay hands upon their head? We are essentially crowning them with whatever you are praying for them about or imparting to them.

These changes can apply to every area of your life. Step into the Court of Crowns and receive what Heaven has, and receive the authority of the Superior Crowns. As sons, demonstrate a superior Kingdom. The time is now!

——— ∞ ———

Chapter 17
Heavenly Assistance

No doubt you could read through the lists of questions under the category of Identifying the False Crowns and identify crowns on many politicians, but we don't just need to look at the politicians. Some blanket prayers will also be needed for the bureaucrats and influencers.

For example, the President surrounds himself with advisors. We want those advisors to provide wise Godly counsel. We want him shielded from those who would provide wicked counsel.

Prophetic Intercessors

We need prophets who can advise our most senior leadership, such as what happened in 2 Kings 6:8-12:

> *⁸ Once when the king of Syria was warring against Israel, he took counsel with his servants,*

saying, 'At such and such a place shall be my camp.'

⁹ But the man of God sent word to the king of Israel, 'Beware that you do not pass this place, for the Syrians are going down there.' ¹⁰ And the king of Israel sent to the place about which the man of God told him. Thus he used to warn him, so that he saved himself there more than once or twice. ¹¹ And the mind of the king of Syria was greatly troubled because of this thing, and he called his servants and said to them, 'Will you not show me who of us is for the king of Israel?'

¹² And one of his servants said, 'None, my lord, O king; but **Elisha, the prophet who is in Israel, tells the king of Israel the words that you speak in your bedroom.'** *(Emphasis mine)*

May these men and women with no agenda other than serving the Father faithfully arise.

Angelic Forces

As we pray for our government officials, we want the angels of Heaven involved. We want the President's angels always ready and on duty, patrolling his bridges and gates and helping him fulfill his scroll.

Fortunately, President Trump has surrounded himself with several Godly men and women in his cabinet and among his other senior leaders. Some of them will be aware of some of the concepts in this book or will, at least, be open to them.

As we engage in this governmental intercession, we will need to activate the angels of the many leaders and commission them to accomplish the will of the Father.

For many, you will need to activate them for the person you are praying for, who may have no concept of angels or of co-laboring with their angels. You can help their angels get activated and duly commissioned.

Realize that some of these people will have angels who need respite. Request backup angels to be assigned until their primary angels are recovered enough to return to duty.

Occasionally, you may need to request replacements for their angels from the Court of Angels, as some may not be able to fulfill their duties sufficiently. If you notice, in your intercessions, someone has constant assaults, and their angels always seem to be bested by the attacks, they either need additional help or replacement, or both. Utilizing their angels to assist in the work is invaluable. This is rare, but you must be aware of the possibility.

In addition, you want your angels to co-labor with the angels assigned to the United States government—the chief angel over America in the Union. There is also the Angel Liberty, not to be confused with Lady Liberty, depicted on some government buildings and the Statue of Liberty. Lady Liberty was recently released from captivity and is on duty. One of the best ways to co-labor with these angels is to pray in the spirit for them. That will help them by providing the direction of Heaven for them.

For our Canadian friends, the Chief Angel over their nation is Dominion. In the northeast portion of the country, the Angel of the Maritimes is on duty. I am unfamiliar with the other angels over the provinces across the country. Often, they will be called by the name of the province. As sons, we want to co-labor with the many angels over the nations. As the names of other angels are determined for states, provinces, or countries, please let me know for our records.

If your governmental intercession is on a state or provincial level, find out the angel's names so you can co-labor with them in a more targeted fashion.

Some readers of this book are called to focus on an international level, while others are called to focus on a national level, others on the state or provincial level, and others on a more local level. Regardless of your focus, as we all fulfill our roles in our assigned places, the principle of Ephesians 4 will be at work where each joint supplies what is needed to build up the whole unit.

These angels are ready to fulfill the Word of the Lord. Many times, they await instructions from the saints. Not every instruction for angels comes directly from Heaven. Some instructions come through the sons who know how to cooperate with Heaven and the Angels.

Patrollers

Patrollers are men and women in white who roam geographical areas like scouts observing the activities in those areas for the sake of information to deliver to the saints. You can read about some in Zechariah 1. You can engage the patrollers over specific areas to gather intelligence on events that require the angels to be released or that require intercession in a particular area. I have more information in my book, *Engaging the Courts for Your City*.[10]

Watchers

Additionally, Heaven has watchers (which are angels who oversee the landscape in a region) assigned to aid in the work. Most teachings about watchers are focused on evil watchers. They perform similar functions, just one for the Kingdom of God and the other for Satan.

---

[10] *Engaging the Courts for Your City* by Dr. Ron M. Horner. LifeSpring Publishing (2019).

These godly watchers can also be consulted for intelligence about the enemy's plans in an area. Don't overlook them. Co-labor with them.

———— ∞ ————

Chapter 18
Fruit Inspectors

As you look at the political landscape, some leaders have given themselves wholly over to many of these false crowns. It is not our aim to judge them, but it is apparent what crowns some are wearing, and it is imperative that we, as sons, know how to intercede for them effectively.

Matthew 12:33:

Either make the tree good and its fruit good, or else make the tree bad and its fruit bad; for a tree is known by its fruit.

The question to ask is, "Whom do we start with?" Ask for the strategy of Heaven. Once you know who your intercession's focus should be, begin identifying what false crowns they are wearing that need to be replaced with Superior Crowns. Part of this whole process will be calling them back to where they should be as sons. Their sin has caused them to miss the mark and forfeit the prize.

They have received a Crown of Authority, as have we all, but what is that crown filled with? Does it have an overflow of the Glory of God, or is it filled with the vileness of hell? Some have made ungodly trades or faced other challenges to achieve their status. We must separate the man or woman from their deeds. We need to see who they are before the family. If we don't love them, stop praying for them. You will pray incorrectly for them. Ask the Father for love for them. Ask Him to help you see them as He sees them.

Jude had this counsel for us to consider in Jude 1:17-23:

> *17 But you, beloved, remember the words which were spoken before by the apostles of our Lord Jesus Christ: 18 how they told you that there would be mockers in the last time who would walk according to their own ungodly lusts.*
>
> *19 These are sensual persons, who cause divisions, not having the Spirit.*
>
> *20 But you, beloved, building yourselves up on your most holy faith, praying in the Holy Spirit, 21* **keep yourselves in the love of God,** *looking for the mercy of our Lord Jesus Christ unto eternal life. 22 And* **on some have compassion, making a distinction;** *23* **but others save with fear, pulling them out of the fire, hating**

even the garment defiled by the flesh. (Emphasis mine)

Those opting for false and inferior crowns haven't been introduced to the goodness of the Father. They don't know Him like you do...yet. Heaven reminded me that there is always grace, but not always mercy. We want to know the difference.

Understanding the significant influences our political leaders face by understanding the false crowns will help us in removing them. Just as the President is under immense pressure, so are the leaders on the other side of the aisle. We want them replaced with godly crowns. We also want to see their Crown of Authority filled with the Glory of Heaven rather than the vileness that some are filled with now. The Body of Christ has done little when it comes to repenting for the sins of our fathers and forefathers. We want God to ignore our sins and answer our prayers anyway, but it does not usually work that way. However, if we are willing to repent, He will answer. We have the promise of 2 Chronicles 7:14 to look to:

> *If My people who are called by My name will humble themselves, and pray and seek My face, and turn from their wicked ways, then I will hear from heaven, and will forgive their sin and heal their land.*

Heaven indicated that although everyone has a Crown of Authority, many have their crown filled with the wrong substance. We want our crowns to be filled with the Glory and substance of the Father. When we see someone, whose crown is contaminated by darkness, we can repent on their behalf, forgive their sins, and request their crown be cleansed and filled with the Glory of Heaven.

When we see someone wearing a Crown of Loathing, we can repent on their behalf, forgive them their sins, and request that the wrap-around love of God be poured into their lives, replacing the Crown of Loathing with a Crown of Grace and a Crown of the Love of the Father.

Those wearing a Crown of Fear, like those with a Crown of Loathing, need it replaced with a Crown of the Wrap-around Love of the Father. Apply these patterns to those wearing the false crowns of the seven-headed dragon, so that they may experience the love and might of God in their lives.

They don't serve God because they don't know God. To know Him is to love Him.

The work of governmental intercession is to align the nation with the purposes of Heaven. Forces have been at work over the last several years to take our nation off course. It's time for the sons to arise, step into the governing role, and legislate from the Courts of Heaven the purposes of God for our nation.

When we, through the perception of our spirit, look at a politician, ask to see what the Father has for them. Regardless of what side of the aisle they sit on, the Father has a plan for their life. Some are precisely where they are supposed to be. Others have been taken off course. May our intercession create a course correction in their life so they can fulfill God's purposes.

———— ∞ ————

Chapter 19
Strategies for Engaging with Angels and Principalities

Our engagement began with the vision of an angel snatching a crown off a principality who said:

> *The effectual fervent prayer of a righteous man avails much.*

Co-laboring with Heaven for this strategy with the angels is imperative to remove this strength that alights upon the heads of the workers of darkness. With crowns comes strength, no matter whose side the wearers are on.

It is not in and of yourselves to pull down principalities, for they are already defeated. However, co-laboring with your angels in this duty to remove the crowns from the derelicts of duty is imperative. For this to be achieved, there must be a release from Heaven.

Do you have a mandate to do so? It is not in and of yourselves, but the angels that remove these crowns. This is a Kingdom principle. It's a dangerous matter to seek to do this yourself. Step into the courts over your region, city, and town, and receive instruction for my people are destroyed for their lack of knowledge (Hosea 4:6). Get a mandate from the Lord and then have the angels strike. Do not put your angels at risk.

Dealing with Poverty in a Region

Your Honor, I request that all books and records regarding those who stood against and prayed in the Courts of Heaven regarding the poverty mentality, including those who have agreed with it and those who have inflicted it. We ask for that to be brought forward in the name of Jesus.

From this place, I ask for the mandate from Heaven to be given to the angels to remove the crown from the spirit of poverty over the region, weaken it, use the capture bags and capture those who come with the spirit of poverty, and judge them in the Courts of Heaven this day.

I ask for the strengthening of the crowns that are needed for my angels and the angels of this region. I commend them to the Father. I do indeed forgive, bless, and release those who have impoverished others, those who have inflicted poverty upon others, and those who have agreed with all of the spirits that come with poverty, laziness, lack, oppression, depression, destruction, innocent bloodshed, and ownership claims.

Thank you for the mandates of Heaven. We ask for the strategic forces in the name of Jesus.

Since the angelic hosts of Heaven can lose their crowns if we put them in a battle in which we haven't received the proper mandate to pull down or remove crowns from principalities. I realize that I must have my crowns in order before we can request the removal of others' crowns. I ask for the authorization of Heaven to be given to the angels assembled to take down the prince(s) and remove their ungodly crowns.

Thank you for the sons who are rising to this challenge.

———— ∞ ————

Chapter 20

Epilogue

Many believers have lost the strength that comes with the crowns they once possessed. In my book, *Embracing Your Crown of Authority*, I discuss how to regain lost, forfeited, or stolen crowns. This book was about understanding the various components within each crown that are ours to maximize. I included a summary of these concepts in this book, as you will need to be able to successfully recover any missing crowns and obtain the others you require.

Since the focus of this book has been governmental intercession, we must know the answer to the following question:

How do we apply the understanding of crowns and governmental intercession?

As we have received our Crown of Authority and our Crown of Governmental Intercession, these will provide the resources to begin the work:

1. Ask Heaven for love for those you are praying for.
2. Gain the strategy of Heaven.
3. Identify the false crowns at work in the lives of those in leadership.
4. Begin the repentance work (use the various Court Scenarios provided in this book).
5. Get the false and ungodly crowns removed from them.
6. Petition Heaven on their behalf for the Superior Crowns of Heaven for them.
7. Get them placed upon their heads.
8. Go to the next person and continue the process.

———— ∞ ————

Appendix

Learning to Live Spirit First

A challenge with how we were taught about the Christian life is that everything was put off until sometime in the future. Then, we read the letters of Paul, and we experienced a disconnect. Heaven, to us, was a destination, not a resource. We knew nothing about learning to live from our spirits. We only knew what we had been doing all our lives since birth, and that was to live to satisfy our soul or our flesh. We sorely need to learn an alternative way of living.

Exchanging Our Way of Living

Paul recorded these words in his letter to the Romans 8:5:

> *Those who are motivated by the flesh only pursue what benefits themselves. But those who live by the impulses of the Holy Spirit are motivated to pursue spiritual realities.*

We must learn to live spirit first! We must exchange our way of living. We must learn to live from our spirit. We need to understand the hierarchy within us:

a. We are a spirit.
b. We possess a soul.
c. We live in a body.

Each component has a specific purpose in our lives. Our spirit is the interface with the supernatural realm. It is designed for interfacing with Heaven and the Kingdom realm. Our spirit has been in existence in our body since conception. Our soul has a different purpose. It communicates to our intellect and our physical body what our spirit has obtained from Heaven. It is the interface with our body. Our body houses the two components and follows the dictates of whichever component is dominating.

Most of us have never been taught about having our spirit dominate. Instead, we have merely assumed that our soul being dominant was the required mode of operation.

Our soul always wants to be in charge. Our soul is susceptible to carnal or fleshly desires, lusts, and behaviors. It will, at times, resist our spirit and body. It must be made to submit to our spirit by an act of our will.

Our will instructs either component (spirit, soul, or body) in what to do. Our soul has a will, and so does our spirit. We choose who dominates!

On the other hand, our body has appetites that will control us in subjection to our soul. They become partners in crime—remember that second piece of chocolate cake it wanted. Our body will try, along with our soul, to dictate our behavior. It will likely resist the spirit's domination of our lives. However, if instructed, it will obey our spirit's domination, and our body can aid our spirit if trained.

The typical expression in most people's lives is that their soul is first, body second, and spirit is somewhere in the distance in last place.

Some people, especially those conscious of their physical fitness or appearance, have a different lineup. Their body is their priority, the soul second, and their spirit is their lowest priority.

Heaven's desire for us is vastly different. Heaven desires that we live spirit first, soul second, and body third. Since we are spiritual beings, this is the optimal arrangement. For most of us, our spirit was not activated in our lives in any measure until we became born again.

If, after our salvation experience, we began to pursue our relationship with the Father, we became much more aware of our spirit and learned to live more spirit-conscious. The apostle Paul wrote in his various epistles about living in the spirit or walking in the spirit.

> *Because we are spiritual beings, our spirits cry out for a deepening of relationship with the Father.*

Our spirit longs for it and will try to steer us in that direction. Many of us had a hunger for God from early in our lives.

Our soul has specific characteristics that explain its behavior in our life. This is the briefest list, but we will get the idea. Our soul is selfish. It wants what it wants when it wants it. It can be very pouty. It can act like a small child. It is offendable and often even looks for opportunities to be offended. Our soul is also rude.

Our body has different sets of characteristics. It is inconsiderate, demanding, lazy, and self-serving. It does not want to get out of bed in the morning, for many people. In others, it wants to be fed things that are not beneficial.

However, the characteristics of our spirits are hugely different. If we live out of our spirit, we will find that we are loving and prone to be gentle. We desire peace. We are considerate. We are far more content when living out of our spirit. Also, joy will often be a significant force in our lives.

Sometimes, we experience traumas that create a situation where our soul does not trust our spirit. The soul blames the spirit for not protecting it. The irony is that, typically, our soul never gave place to the spirit so that it could protect us. The soul places false blame on the spirit, and it must be coerced to forgive the spirit. Then, the soul must relinquish control to the spirit. Once the soul forgives the spirit, the two components can work in harmony.

What would happen if I were to flash an image of some delicious, freshly cooked donuts in front of us? For many, their body would announce a craving for one. What if I showed an image of a bowl of broccoli instead? How many people would get excited about that? Probably not as much excitement over a bowl of broccoli would be exhibited. Which does our body prefer, donuts or broccoli? The donuts are likely to win out for the untamed soul every time. Which do most kids prefer?

In any case, we can train ourselves to choose the healthier option. A principle regarding this that I heard years ago is summed up like this:

What we feed will live—
what we starve will die

What do we want to be dominant—our spirit, soul, or body? The part we feed is the part that will dominate.

Some feed their soul and live by the logic of their mind. Everything must be reasoned out in their mind before they will accept it. However, because our soul gains insight from the Tree of the Knowledge of Good and Evil, it will always have faulty and limited understandings.

How do we change this soul-dominant or body-dominant pattern? We instruct our soul to back up and call our spirit to come forward. Some people may need to physically stand up and speak to their soul and say, "Soul, back up." As they say those words, they take a physical step backward. Then, talk to their spirit out loud and say, "Spirit, come forward." As we speak those words, take a physical step forward. This prophetic act helps trigger a shift within them.

Live spirit first!

Benefits of Living Spirit First

Why would we want to live spirit first? Let me present several reasons. Living spirit first will create an increased awareness of Heaven and the realms of Heaven. It will make a deeper comprehension of the presence of Holy Spirit, angels, and men and women in white linen. We will be able to hear the voice of Heaven better. We will experience greater creativity, productivity, hope, and peace. We will become more aware of the needs of people that we meet.

*As we live spirit first,
we will be able to access
the riches of Heaven in our life.*

Petty things that formerly bothered us will dissipate in importance or impact on our lives. We can move ahead, not concerned with the petty, mundane, or unproductive things that have affected our lives before we begin to live spirit first.

This way of life is more than a game changer—for the believer, it is the only way to live. We will face challenges as we build our business or live from Heaven down. Still, we will more readily be able to access the solutions of Heaven as we live with an awareness of the richness of Heaven and all that is available to us as a son or daughter of the Lord Most High. Do not live dominated by the soul.

*Live **spirit** first!*

∞

Petitions for Divorce

The Petitions for Divorce in the following two sections are available in the book *Divorced!* by Jeanette Strauss & Doug Carr (edited by Dr. Ron M. Horner). The prayers in the book are in forms modified for Individuals, Families, Businesses, Churches and Ministries, and Regions and Territories.

———— ∞ ————

Petitions for Divorce from the Sun God & the Moon God

Many reading this book are familiar with the Baal Divorce decree popularized by Apostle John Benefiel of the Heartland Apostolic Prayer Network (hapn.org). The revelation that we have indeed been "married" to the principality Baal (even if unknowingly) and have a need to be divorced from that entity has had a tremendous impact in many lives. However, I have come to realize recently that although the divorce decree has had some effect, in many instances its impact has been limited.

God considered the children of Israel to be married to Him, and any interference in that marriage was never taken lightly by God. When the children of Israel entered into covenants with unbelievers (whether by marriage or otherwise), it created a "marriage" that God did not approve of. God viewed adultery as a breaking of faith with him. It should come as no surprise that He would provide a venue through which healing can come to this most important of covenants.

The Hebrew word *na-aph* figuratively means to apostatize. We use apostasy to indicate one who has broken faith with God. God continually warned the Israelites not to get into covenant relationships with unbelievers.

Apostolic Prayer Leaders Jeanette Strauss & Doug Carr graciously permitted us to use the Petition of Divorce from the Sun God (Baal) and the Moon God (Allah). They are thorough but will bring great benefits to your life.

———— ∞ ————

Petition of Divorce from the Sun God

My strategy to win this case is based upon repentance, forgiveness, and restoration to God. I will request a divorce from Baal and marriage to The Lord.

Opening Prayer

Dear Heavenly Father, thank You for the summons You sent to me through the Holy Spirit requesting that I, as an individual, appear before You in the courtroom of Heaven on behalf of this family.

I am honored to come together in agreement representing myself.

Thank You for this opportunity to bring my case into the courtroom of Heaven.

I ask that my record book be opened and the Judge look back to the beginning of my creation.

I ask that all previous righteous, intercessory prayers that have been presented to You on my behalf throughout the past generations be included with my petitions. Amen.

This Scripture found in Isaiah 58:12 describes my intention:

Those from among You shall build the old waste places; You shall raise up the foundations of many generations; and You shall be called the Repairer of the breach, The Restorer of streets to dwell in.

Through the power of the Holy Spirit combined with my prayers, I can play a part as a restorer of the breach in my life. I am called to be an Ambassador of Reconciliation and am endowed with the power of attorney through the authority of Jesus Christ, whom he has delegated to me as a believer.

I understand that the power and authority to change my community and transform my territory come from the Righteous Judge of Heaven and Earth, who presides over the Courts of Heaven. When I legally settle my case in Heaven's court, I can expect a corresponding action on Earth.

The Holy Spirit has brought to my attention that the trials and tribulations I read about and experience daily in this family have grown out of a rotten root of disobedience and rebellion to the ways of God, which has been growing for years and has obtained a spiritual legal right to grow into a large tree that has been bearing bad fruit in this family. I understand and admit that this is due to sin committed against You. This is why I look forward to coming into Your courtroom in Heaven on behalf of this family and laying the ax to the root.

One of my focuses is to divorce the foreign god, Baal, in all his forms. I am using information from Chuck Pierce and Dutch Sheets Ministries that pertain to this case, which can also be found on the Heartland Apostolic Prayer Network website (www.hapn.org).

My first question is: "Who is my enemy, Baal, and how is he affecting me today?"

Chuck and Dutch say:

> *Baal is identified as the ruler of the demons. Matthew 12:24 (Beel-ze-bub is another name for Baal). Baal-hamon, one of his names, means "the lord of wealth or abundance." This is the principality warring against the great transfer of wealth to the church. You must war against this spirit to see your inheritance released.*
>
> *Baal-berith, another of his names, means "the lord of the covenant." The Hebrew word Baal means "husband" or "marriage." This spirit always attempted to cause Israel to "divorce" or break covenant with God and "marry" or align with him. Consistent with this, in so many ways America has broken its covenant with God and married Baal. This is, I believe, the strongman behind most covenant-breaking.*

Baal is the strongman behind sexual perversion. Homosexuality was and is one of his great strongholds. I believe all of the sexual sin and perversion in America is, to one degree or another, under Baal's orchestration. You will continue to see God expose leaders in the church who have aligned themselves with this spirit. Pray for the church to be cleansed and for Baal's hold on America in this area to be broken.

Baal always goes after the next generation, trying to cut off the extension of God's covenantal purposes. He is a violent spirit and even required human sacrifice. Abortion is under Baal, as is the "cutting" of today's young generation. (See 1 Kings 18:28.)

I agree this includes the Vampire and Goth movement, and the death culture that has so invaded America. Baal is leading the fight to avert the great awakening planned for the young generation of Americans today. I must pray against them and see that these efforts are bound. Witchcraft and occult spirits, in general, operate under Baal, as does Jezebel.

The Baal Principality (god of 1,000 faces) Baal (Sun god): Bel, Apollo, Zeus, Marduk, Ahura-Mazda, Osiris, Tammuz, Dagon, Prometheus, Jupiter, Nimrod, Mithra ("Another Jesus" and "The Anti-Christ"), Ra, Lucetius, Dyaus, Dionysus, Hermes, Adonis, Pan, Hades, Eros,

Uranus, Gaea, Assur, Merodach, Ninus, Shamas, Zeus-Belus, Bacchus Queen of Heaven (Moon & Sun goddess): Mother of Harlots, Mother of God (and child), The Great Mother, Ashtaroth, Artemis, Aphrodite, Juno, Lilith, Minerva, Columbia, Nike, Astarte, Athena, Beltis, Diana, Isis (Horus), Anahita, Inanna, Tanat, Ishtar (Easter), Cybele, Mylitta, Hathor, Kali, Columbia Leviathan: Neptune, Poseidon, Tiamet, King of Children of Pride ministry.

My strategy to gain the victory over this principality is through courtroom of Heaven intercession. I will obtain the legal right through repentance and forgiveness for sin committed against God to remove the lawful rights Baal has used to withhold the transfer of wealth and release my inheritance. Chuck Pierce tells me to claim Jeremiah 51:44 which I will include in my decrees.

I have subtitled each of the prayer point issues listed above with the numbers 1-4. I will list the problem, then my repentance and forgiveness prayer; in conclusion, I will present my plea for resolution and court-ordered restitution.

I understand the importance of praying in unity as I present my plea. One of the best ways to do this is to pray the prayer Jesus told me to pray corporately. This prayer is found in Matthew 6:9-13 and will spiritually cleanse me of unrighteousness so I can stand before the Judge to present my petitions.

Let's join together and pray the model prayer (using sin and sins instead of trespass and trespasses).

> *[9] My Father in Heaven, may Your name be kept holy. [10] May Your Kingdom come soon. May Your will be done on earth, as it is in Heaven. [11] Give me today the food I need, [12] and forgive me of my sins, as I have forgiven those who sin against me. [13] And don't let me yield to temptation, but rescue me from the evil one. (Matthew 6:9-13) (NLT)*

Let me go into the courtroom now and present the case.

Thank You for the honor of allowing me to come into Your courtroom. I know the form of intercession. You always endorse and grant favor upon is when Your people recognize their wicked ways, humble themselves, and repent. You then extend forgiveness, grace, and mercy and will release healing.

I want to present this Scripture as evidence of Your faithfulness:

2 Chronicles 7:14:

> *If My people who are called by My name will humble themselves, and pray and seek My face, and turn from their wicked ways, then I will hear from Heaven, and will forgive their sin and heal their land.*

I thank You that in the Bible, You welcome and encourage me to come into Your courtroom and state my case. As I repent and ask forgiveness, I can get the records cleared, and You are willing to defend me and help me win my spiritual battles, which will give me the victory in the physical realm.

You say in Isaiah 43:25-26:

> *²⁵ I, even I, am He who blots out Your transgressions for My own sake, and I will not remember Your sins. ²⁶ Put Me in remembrance; let us contend together; state Your case, that You may be acquitted.*

I thank You for subpoenaeing the accuser of the brethren so that he can be a witness today to these divorce proceedings.

In this case, today, I use as an example and reference point of proper intercession that found on behalf of Your people in Daniel 9:10.

Daniel found himself as a slave who was a believer, living in a Babylonian society with no rights to worship his God freely the way that he wanted to. He didn't complain to God about the injustice but humbled himself, repented, and asked forgiveness for his sins and the sins of the nation of Israel. God listened and acted on his behalf.

At this time, I come before You as Daniel did, in humble repentance. I do not come before Your bench to complain about injustices against me for what my forefathers were guilty of. I am not here to take the role of the accuser of what they did wrong, but I am here to repent for a turning away from Godly ordinances and statutes and living in disobedience and rebellion to my God. I ask that it be placed in the record that I forgive them for their actions, which have caused consequences and repercussions that I am struggling with today.

I ask that the intercession for my family and all of its issues connected to these different forms of Baal all be put into one case, a class action suit. I know the accuser or prosecuting attorney (ha-satan) has been convicting me of sin and getting judgments against me and the people connected to this family, which has placed this family and its members in bondage.

I don't know precisely when this marriage of the perversion of truth began in history. Still, I am asking that the record go back to the earliest foundation or the original place where the turning away and embracing the doctrine of demons began and include every violation up to now.

Prayer Point 1

[Matthew 12:24 reveals that Beelzebub is another name for Baal. Baal-hamon, one of Baal's names, means "the lord of wealth or abundance." Dutch Sheets and Chuck Pierce agree that this is the principality warring against the great transfer of wealth to the church. I must effectively overcome this spirit to see my inheritance released.]

Charge 1

The Accuser's Argument Against Me

He has sinned by investing in the kingdom of darkness in many ways that I, the deceiver and accuser, have cleverly devised to obtain guilty verdicts against him/her. Therefore, I have been able to get a judgment to get their inheritance withheld from them.

The strength that I use against You and them is because they break Your laws.

1 Corinthians 15:56 says:

> *The sting of death is sin, and the strength of sin is the law.*

My Response to the Charge

Your Honor, I admit my guilt, and I stand on my behalf, repenting for the sin of investing any money through the products I buy and the businesses that I allow to come into this region such as casinos that help to promote the activities of this principality named Baal and give him the right to steal my finances.

I ask that You forgive my sin and cover me with the Blood of Jesus. I request that the Freedom of Information Act be applied to this case. That truth will be revealed at a personal level to those who are being deceived. I ask that all corruption be exposed and dealt with to bring about Godly change in my life.

As the Freedom of Information is loosed over my inheritance, which consists of people and those You have called to come out of the darkness, the scales over the eyes of my understanding and their understanding will fall away. The veils of deception will be cast off. I will see Your truth, embrace Your truth, and walk in Your truth.

Please move this case that the enemy has been lawfully binding me to, and thereby enforcing judgments against me from the Courtroom of Heaven to the throne of Your Grace and Mercy, loosing me and others whom he has been holding captive through sin, removing the legal rights of Baal and any other foreign god involved in this hindrance.

I petition You to release my inheritance and the great transfer of wealth You have in reserve for Your church. My accuser will no longer have a case. He has to release the captives.

Jeremiah 51:44 states:

> **I will punish and judge Bel (or Baal) [the handmade god] in Babylon and take out of his mouth what he has swallowed up [the stolen sacred articles and the captives of Judah and elsewhere].** *The nations will no longer flow to him. Yes, the wall of Babylon has fallen down! (AMP)*

Prayer Point 2

[Baal-berith, another of his names, means "the lord of the covenant." The Hebrew word Baal means "husband" or "marriage." This spirit always attempted to cause Israel to "divorce" or break covenant with God and "marry" or align with him. Consistent with this, in so many ways, America has broken its covenant with God and married Baal. This is the strongman behind most covenant-breaking.]

Charge 2

The Accuser's Argument Against Me

Many of those who call themselves by the name of the Lord God Most High have repeatedly committed spiritual adultery against You by not taking Your ordinances and laws seriously. Many are guilty of committing adultery amongst themselves or participating in pornography, so I can prosecute them for their sin of breaking covenant with You and with each other. I capture them through their sin and entice them through many devious means to break the covenant in their earthly marriages.

My Response to the Charge

I admit to this sin that has influenced me as an individual and even as a nation. My adversary has been successful in his quest to divide and effectively move me out from under Your covenant protection due to sin which opens the door for him in my life. He is at work destroying my covenant relationships with others and between You and me. Government statistics on the divorce rate prove that he has been successful.

Personal Confession

I repent and ask forgiveness for my great sin against You and others. I ask that You cover this sin I have committed with the blood of Jesus.

I petition for a judgment declaring the granting of an immediate termination of this marriage to Baal. I request a divorce, a cutting off from him in every area.

I ask You to grant a season of time during which You will release a spirit of revelation of truth and conviction upon me, during which time my understanding will be opened and my heart made ready for the Gospel in full measure. I also request a spirit of repentance that will bring a harvest of salvations and born-again experiences to my region.

I pray for a revival of Your Holy Spirit and the gifts of the Holy Spirit to manifest, which will assist in the harvest. I ask that You grant me insight and wisdom as You manifest Your presence in a greater way in my midst. Amen.

I agree with 1 John 1:9:

If I confess my sins, He is faithful and just to forgive me my sins and to cleanse me from all unrighteousness.

I am the Bride of Christ. I ask for my marriage to Jesus Christ to be reestablished. I understand I am being cleansed and restored to my rightful place of honor before my king. I agree to turn my heart fully toward the plans and purposes You have for me. I am dedicated to performing Your will for my life, agreeing to the transformation process that You have planned, which will seal me as a covenantal people with You.

Prayer Point 3

[Baal is the strongman behind sexual perversion. Homosexuality was and is one of his significant strongholds. I believe all of the sexual sin and perversion in America is, to one degree or another, under Baal's orchestration. I will continue to see God expose leaders in the church who have aligned themselves with this spirit. I pray for the church to be cleansed and for Baal's hold on America in this area to be broken.]

The Accuser's Argument Against Me

There may be times when he/she doesn't care about what the Bible or the Judge in this courtroom has to say about homosexuality or other forms of what the Bible says is sexual perversion. He/she even calls him/ themselves a Christian.

I have been able to spread my perversion in many ways through most forms of media. My agenda is marching on. This state is passing laws including the legality of homosexual marriage, which is my counterfeit marriage arrangement. Laws are being passed in favor of all kinds of gay and lesbian rights. Even church leaders are turning away from the truth. My goal is for you to give them up to me. Your Word is clear: this lifestyle is a sin.

As evidence, I present Romans 1:26-28:

> [26] *For this reason God gave them up to vile passions. For even their women exchanged the natural use for what is against nature.* [27] *Likewise also the men, leaving the natural use of the woman, burned in their lust for one another, men with men committing what is shameful, and receiving in themselves the penalty of their error which was due.* [28] *And even as they did not like to retain God in their*

> *knowledge, God gave them over to a debased mind, to do those things which are not fitting.*

So you see that I am working within my legal jurisdiction.

My Response

I agree that the accuser has been at work in me. I also aim to remove his legal rights from me in this area. I know I can do this through repentance and asking for forgiveness. I stand in the gap right now repenting on behalf of the sin I have committed against You by living and promoting the homosexual, gay and lesbian, transgender lifestyle. I ask forgiveness for this great abomination toward You.

Personal Confession

I thank You, Lord, that You plan to turn this into a testimony for Your goodness and mercy.

I, like Jeremiah, was sealed by You before I was born.

Jeremiah 1:5 says:

> *I knew You before I formed You in Your mother's womb. Before You were born, I set You apart and appointed You as my prophet to the nations.*

I remind You now of those who, according to Your Word, are in the camp of the enemy as captives. I petition You for all those who have been stolen from Your purposes. I petition You, Lord, to send Your host to recover Your lost children.

Jeremiah 3:22 says:

> *'My wayward children,' says the LORD, 'come back to me, and I will heal Your wayward hearts." "Yes, we're coming," the people reply, "for You are the LORD my God.' (NLT)*

I also target my petition toward those who are now promoting the homosexual agenda and who have large media platforms. I petition You and thank You ahead of time for bringing them into the Kingdom of God.

Your will is that none perish but have everlasting life. Lord, help them in their unbelief. I set my faith that they will be saved, born-again, and filled with the Holy Spirit. Their lives will be turned around to promote the truth and a Godly agenda and be used to set countless numbers free.

I find it interesting that they have chosen the rainbow as their object of identification. According to Your Word, the rainbow is Your symbol given to me of Your faithfulness. I decree that this is a prophetic statement they are waving over themselves. By their actions, as they wave their banners, they claim a restoration to a Godly covenant over their lives. I can be encouraged that You will be faithful, cleanse them of sin, and restore them to their rightful place in Your Kingdom.

I ask you to perform an emergency intervention, as you can only orchestrate it.

I ask for forgiveness and washing with the blood of Jesus over this terrible sin.

I ask that I be moved from judgment to the throne of Grace and Mercy where You will extend a season of grace and mercy over me so that the laws can be changed.

Help show me what to do to get these perverse laws repealed from the books.

Prayer Point 4

[Baal always goes after the next generation, trying to cut off the extension of God's covenantal purposes. He is a violent spirit and even requires human sacrifice. Abortion is under Baal, as is the "cutting" of today's young generation (see 1 Kings 18:28), the Vampire and Goth movement, and the death culture, in general, that has so invaded America. Baal is leading the fight to avert the great awakening planned for the young generation of Americans today. Pray against and get these efforts bound. Witchcraft and occult spirits, in general, operate under Baal. So does Jezebel.]

The Accuser's Argument Against Me

He says:

I am working within my authority. This region allows legalized abortion by state law. I have been able to cut out whole generations legally. This is a form of human sacrifice that I am promoting today. I am stealing the youth of this region for my purposes. My witchcraft and occult promotion projects are going well. Most people don't bother me as I go about my business.

My Response

As a believer, I am grieved by the legalization of abortion. As a taxpayer, I share in the blood guilt that cries out for judgment. I can see the hand of my accuser using this legalization also to attempt to kill the youth off through suicide, drug use, or other means.

Personal Confession

I repent on behalf of the sin of abortion and ask forgiveness for that sin.

I repent for the loss of destinies and purposes that have occurred in the earth as a result of this great sin.

I ask that You hear my plea and help me move my case from judgment to grace and mercy for a season in time where You will help me employ strategies to change my laws. Bless and promote the agenda and finances of those fighting to change these laws. Remove the veils off of my lawmakers' and voters' eyes, and empower me by Your Holy Spirit to support the move to get my laws changed so abortion will no longer be legal.

I ask You to invade the camp of the enemy with Your Host of Heaven. Arrest and prosecute those who are practicing and promoting witchcraft and the occult in my region. I am standing in the gap, repenting for this sin in my region and asking forgiveness. I ask for Your Glory to invade my region, wash me clean, and heal my heart, mind, and land. Amen.

> [I have a representative from the younger generation who would like to offer a plea in court.]

Ambassador of the Younger Generation

Dear Jesus, I stand before You as a representative for those who are of this younger generation. I humbly stand in the gap, repenting for the sins that are recorded as charges against me in the courtroom of Heaven. I especially ask forgiveness for the sin of rebellion and disobedience I have committed against You, my parents, and those in authority over me, which has allowed a curse to come upon me.

I forgive my parents and others who have sinned against me. I ask for a spirit of reconciliation and healing to come *upon me. I ask You to turn the hearts of the fathers to their children and the children's hearts to their fathers.*

I thank You, Father God, that Your Word says children are a heritage and a gift from You. You say the fruit of the womb is Your reward. I stand in the gap repenting on behalf of the sin of abortion among the younger generation and ask forgiveness for that sin which has given the enemy a legal right to go after this generation.

Our enemy is blinding me to the truth due to my sin. He has placed a veil over the eyes of my understanding. Some of Your children are overwhelmed with discouragement, believing the lie that says they can't get out of bondage they are under. This is causing untimely deaths of young people through drug overdose, suicide, and self-hatred.

I ask You for a spirit of salvation to be loosed in my region for my younger generation. Help me to be fruitful for Your Kingdom. As I am forgiven for my sins, cover me with the Blood of Jesus Christ. Stir up the gifts of the Holy Spirit among me. Baptize me with a new baptism of fire that will burn out all the bondages and set me on fire for Your Word. Please move the enemy's case against me to the Throne of Grace and Mercy.

I ask You to place me in protective custody during the season in which You will remove the veils and scales from off of my eyes, and I will see the truth, embrace the truth, and walk in Your truth. Amen.

I confess what You say You will do for me in Isaiah 49:24-25:

> *²⁴ Shall the prey be taken from the mighty, or the captives of the righteous be delivered? ²⁵ But thus says the LORD: "Even the captives of the mighty shall be taken away, and the prey of the terrible be delivered; for I will contend with him who contends with You, and I will save Your children.*

Thank You for hearing my plea on behalf of the younger generation and answering my prayer as You answered Daniel, a man of the younger generation.

I will read the answer to Daniel as he prayed as I have prayed.

Daniel 9:20-23:

> *²⁰ Now while I was speaking, praying, and confessing my sin and the sin of my people Israel, and presenting my supplication before the LORD my God for the holy mountain of my God, ²¹ yes, while I was speaking in prayer, the man Gabriel, whom I had seen in the vision at the beginning, being caused to fly swiftly, reached me about the time of the evening offering. ²² And he informed me, and talked with me, and said, "O Daniel, I have now come forth to give you skill to understand. ²³ At the beginning of your supplications the command went out, and I have come to tell you, for you are greatly beloved;*

therefore, consider the matter, and understand the vision.

I remind You and remember the results of Daniel's prayers of intercession. I agree with Your Word that says:

Your purpose shall be established, and You will do all that pleases You for me. This applies to me today.

Psalm 103:20 says the angels hearken to the voice of the Word and go forth to perform it. As I have presented my repentance and received forgiveness, then quoted the Word after each point; the angels present heard the voice of the Word and are going forth to perform it in this family.

Isaiah 46:9-10 says:

> *[9] Remember the former things of old, for I am God, and there is no other; I am God, and there is none like Me, [10] declaring the end from the beginning, and from ancient times things that are not yet done, saying, "My counsel shall stand, and I will do all My pleasure."*

Facilitator

That concludes my prayer petitions and decrees portion of the courtroom session concerning the 4 prayer points I was instructed to present for this family. I know, according to 1 John 5:14-15, that the divorce decree has been granted to me as an individual, and I have reestablished my covenant with the King of Kings, Jesus Christ, my Bridegroom.

Before I conclude, I still have some courtroom business to attend to.

Addressing My Accuser

Now, the Judge will ask me if I have anything to say to my accuser, and I respond by saying, "Yes, Your Honor. I will quote Your Word to Him, which is high praise to Your ears, and by doing this, I will make him Your footstool."

Personal Confession

The Lord says that my adversaries shall be clothed with shame.

You shall cover yourself with confusion as with a mantle.

My Lord says in His Word that His hand shall find every one of my enemies; He shall make you as a fiery oven in His anger.

He shall swallow you in His wrath, and His fire shall devour you.

Your fruit shall be destroyed from the land, and your bad seed from among the children of men.

You have intended evil against me; you imagined a mischievous device you cannot perform.

My Father will destroy your schemes and confuse your tongues.

You shall be confounded and put to shame.

You shall be turned back and brought to confusion because you have devised my hurt.

You shall be as chaff before the wind, and the angel of the Lord shall chase you.

Your way will be dark and slippery, and the angel of the Lord shall persecute you.

My Father says in His Word, Behold, I will plead your case and take vengeance for you. Psalm 109:29; Psalm 21:8-11; Psalm 55:9; Jeremiah 51:36.

I thank my Father, the Righteous Judge, Jesus the Son, and the Holy Spirit for hearing my case and ruling in my favor.

Scriptures to Quote to the Judge Corporately

Lord God, You have established Your throne in Heaven, and Your Kingdom rules over all.

For You, Lord, are my Judge and Lawgiver; You are my King; You will save me.

Our soul shall be joyful in You. I shall rejoice in Your salvation.

Be exalted, oh Lord, in Your strength. I will sing and praise Your great power.

I thank You, Father, for Your great mercies that You have not withheld from me.

May Your loving kindness and truth continually preserve me.

Thank Jesus for making it possible for me to enter the courtroom of Heaven and plead my case.

Dear Jesus, thank You for Your loving sacrifice for me. You died so I could be free.

I will strive with the help of the Holy Spirit to walk in love toward others as You loved me,

I will not judge and extend grace and mercy as You extend grace and mercy to me daily.

I ask that I could become more like You every day. When others see me, they will see You.

Help me to desire the meat of Your Word, which, as I read it, I will be washed clean. Teach me Your ways.

Thank You, Lord, for listening and helping me walk deeper in faith and be bolder in prayer. Bless Your Holy Name. Amen.

Thank You, Holy Spirit; I thank You for Your presence on this earth. You surround me with Your presence; You inhabit my being.

You comfort and encourage me during times of trouble in my life.

You bring divine revelation to me as I need it. You bring all things to remembrance to my mind.

You reveal treasure hidden in deep places when I least expect it, especially Scriptures that I have read in the past but can't recall.

You have perfect recall and love to help me out, and I thank You for that.

You are the light within me that releases Your Glory and casts out darkness.

Thank You for lighting my path and divinely directing me every day.

Bless You for all You do that I do not recognize as Your work. Amen.

> [Now, step into the Court of Scribes and obtain the verdict just rendered, then step into the Court of Angels and request angelic dispatch for the orders and instructions of the verdict rendered.]

Apostolic Blessing

May the Lord bless me, members of the Kingdom of God, and bride of Jesus Christ, with His blessings as I keep my marital commitment to Christ by abiding in Him, submitting to Him, and honoring Him with sincere reverence and humble service.

I declare that as I submit to His lead, He will submit to my need. Bless me, Father, with full marital rights, which will impregnate me with vision, leading to holiness and multiplication. I ask You this day to translate me from shame to favor.

Bless me, I pray, as I seek Your face. Amen.

> [Now that you have received a verdict, you will want to access the Court of Scribes for the verdict and for any additional scrolls. You will then take them into the Court of Angels for dispatch.

———— ∞ ————

Petition of Divorce from the Moon God

(also called the sin god)

In divorcing the moon god, we are completing the necessary divorce procedures. The Divorce from Baal (the sun god) coupled with the Divorce from the Moon god (allah) should bring you into a new level of freedom in your life. This also can be applied to your region or territory.

On the following pages, you will read the various ways the moon god has impacted our lives and how it got entrance into our lives. Interspersed in the teachings by Jeanette Strauss and Doug Carr are prayers of repentance as well as petitions. When performing these prayers in a group, the Compiled Prayers section contains only the prayers of repentance and petitions.

May you enjoy new levels of freedom in your life from this day forward.

Jeanette Strauss, an apostolic prayer leader in Michigan, working with Apostle Doug Carr, was responsible for the Divorce Decree from Baal, which you may have already seen. That specific decree resulted from a prayer event they convened on behalf of their geographic region and led Jeanette to do more research. Here is what she had to say:

> *That case was settled, and the highest court granted the divorce. After praying and seeking God to see if any further actions needed attention, we sensed the Lord leading us to examine who the moon god is. Baal is known as the sun god, so that covers 12 hours of the day, but who is the moon god who rules the night? We considered who he was and what he influenced, and we were determined to also seek a divorce from him.*
>
> *We discovered one of his names is 'sin.' Another more familiar name to us is 'allah.' Different Arab tribes gave the Moon god different names/titles. Some of the names/titles for this moon god are 'Sin, Hubul, Ilumquh, Al-ilah.' The word 'allah' is derived from 'al-ilah'[11] allah and is identified by the symbol of the crescent moon and the star.*

---

[11] http://www.bible.ca/islam/islam-moon-god.htm

When we hear the name allah, our minds might go to the Muslim nations and their symbol of the crescent and star, or even the name of their god allah, which is the same god as the sin god. We tend to think this is the god of the Middle East region, but Americans are tied in a very real and active way to this moon god.

Apostolic leader Doug Carr joins in:

The Lord opened portals of revelation for me as I prayer walked on in mid-April a few years ago. The moon was very bright, and I could see the road, the outline of trees and shrubs, and the silhouette of geese on the river. I knew I was walking in the lesser light of the moon rather than the greater light given to govern the day. Even before I started walking, I sensed how the moon god tries to deceive individuals and regions to walk in his lesser light.

As Baal is god of the sun, Allah is the god of the moon. God created the moon as the lesser light to govern the night. Sin and Satan have defiled such governance, so people, including Christians, are often governed by the lesser light of darkness rather than by seeking and walking in the Light of God the Father, God the Son, and God the Holy Spirit.

The moon god(s) cause us to walk in lesser light. Under his influence:

- *We do not seek God's light on WHY things are the way they are.*
- *We settle for less than the best, giving in to entitlement's bondage rather than seeking God's solutions for poverty, violence, hatred, and the like.*
- *We submit to oppressive rule rather than seek the greater light and freedom from Jehovah Himself. This is true of nations under dictatorial rule, as well as individuals under dictatorial rule in homes, churches, society, and workplaces.*
- *People under the influence of the moon god would rather have other people fix their problems, even if it leads to bondage, rather than seek solutions from the Lord.*

The mood god hinders people from seeking God's Greater Light through:

- *The Word of God (2 Timothy 2:15, 3:16-17)*
- *The Wisdom (heavenly wisdom) of God (James 1:8; 3:13-18)*
- *The World of Revelation (voice of creation) (Romans 1:20b)*

Sluggards do not go to the ant to learn how to be self-sufficient. Instead, they rely on others to rescue them and provide for their needs: Rather than asking God how to take better care of their bodies, they expect doctors or faith healers to repair the damage they bring on themselves, etc. (Proverbs 6:6-11)

The twofold witness of God is the voice of conscience (Romans 1:20a) and the inner voice of adoption. (Romans 8:15)

People look to others for personal revelation rather than to God. Rather than seek God for themselves, they rely on prophets and the Elijah List or other means.

Ways the Moon God Works

The Moon God Exploits the Power of Secrecy

By keeping things hidden (occult, Masonic, etc.), the moon god is able to continue sin patterns and destroy lives. We see family secrets as well as church secrets. A pastor is a perpetrator, but rather than disciplining the perpetrator, they excommunicate the victim.

In another church, a gay pastor who oversees a daycare was accused of inappropriate behavior. Rather than addressing the inappropriate behavior of the pastor against children in a church daycare, the church fired those trying to address the concerns.

The Moon God Partners with Allah

The Moon god partners with Allah to make people passive so they will not seek God for their answers. Rather than seeking why sickness lingers, they expect medicine or faith healers to take care of their problems. Rather than learning to resist the devil and make him flee, they expect deliverance ministers to fix them.

The Moon God Seduces

Moon god seduces believers to hide SIN and secretly continue in it rather than confess it and repent of it.

The Moon God Oppresses Women

The Moon god oppresses women and covers their beauty and potential in life and ministry.

The Moon God Distracts

The moon god covers the power of a multitude of sins by distracting focus from personal responsibility. A few terrorists bomb two churches on Palm Sunday, and the whole world reacts because of the magnitude of the damage. Around forty-nine people were killed, and one hundred were injured. Compare that to the multitude of people under the influence of moon gods in local churches. They expect someone else to provide for their families, their medical needs, their housing, their education, and everything else from birth to burial. Their mistaken allegiance to the agenda of the moon god goes unnoticed. By the power of being hidden, these deities destroy more churches, families, neighborhoods, and communities than the ISIS terrorists behind the church bombings. These deities continue to rob, steal, and destroy families, communities, and nations because they passively give in to the seduction of the moon god rather than seeking the greater light of Christ. We will cover any connection we may have to this lesser light moon god before we conclude our court case.

These important issues that occur due to living in this lesser light and other symptoms of the curse due to the moon god being active in our generational bloodlines are what we will take action on. Not only are many walking and struggling along in the lesser light. not understanding what is really going on, but many believers have been unwittingly snared and are being harassed by this moon god.

Being a Legal Heir

Some are suffering adverse consequences due to someone in their bloodline who pledged themselves to this foreign god by decreeing certain required oaths and vows of faithfulness to this god without fully realizing what they were doing. We are speaking of the different organizations of secrecy that people can think are a good thing because they do good things to help people, and they display a lot of religious articles so people can be deceived. They use crosses in their ceremonies as well as Bibles.

Pledges of Loyalty unto Death

Most of us understand that if a vow is sworn to a foreign god, this brings a curse that allows demons the right to attack the person involved and their bloodline. Some of you here may recognize symptoms of illnesses or physical afflictions that have become resident in your families as you read the oaths and vows a relative may have spoken over themselves when joining one of these organizations that are under the jurisdiction of the moon god allah; these oaths require a person to pledge their complete loyalty to the point of death.

A Curse Without Cause

The Word says that a curse can come on a person if it has a legal right or a cause. These curses will exercise their legal right to light and attach firmly, then begin the journey down the generational bloodline. It will only be stopped effectively when the root cause is repented for and forgiven by God, and then the curse is revoked.

> *Like a flitting sparrow, like a flying swallow, So a curse without cause shall not alight. (Proverbs 26:2)*

Prayer of Repentance

Let us begin by praying a corporate prayer of repentance, in general, but not a specific prayer for now. This is important to do before we get into facts, in this case, against the moon god. It is possible that the enemy has a veil over our eyes, and we cannot see the deception we could be struggling under, so we do this so veils come off before we begin.

> *Dear Heavenly Father, I stand before You today in the Courtroom in Heaven. I repent on behalf of any sin I have committed against You or Your Word. I confess my sins and ask You to forgive me and cover them over with the blood of Jesus. I ask You to move any case the enemy presents against me to the Throne of Grace and Mercy, where the Lord will remove any veils that may be over the eyes of my understanding, and I will see the truth, and it will set me free. Amen.*

...

As we present our case, we are covering our generational bloodlines. Like Daniel in the Bible, we are called to be Ambassadors of Reconciliation for our region, territory, and families. We do this on behalf of those who do not know what has been spoken over them or, in their ignorance, have spoken these vows and oaths themselves and been ensnared by this god, which has affected our lives. Holy Spirit will guide a person into all truth. It is not our job to bring people into account; instead, our job is to intercede.

We can find ourselves ensnared if we or our ancestors have been or still are members of any of these organizations: Freemasonry, Shriners, Eastern Star, Prince Hall Lodge, or any other secret society, including fraternities and sororities. The validation this curse uses is the verbal oaths and vows that establish spoken covenants, followed by symbolic enactment to confirm the pledge of commitment and devotion that we or someone in our generational bloodline performs.

Technically, these vows and enactments have been spoken and performed in front of God and witnesses, just as marriage vows are. Those marriage vows are legally in force and binding until a divorce is legalized. The Bible says:

Proverbs 6:2:

You are snared by the words of your mouth; you are taken by the words of your mouth.

Matthew 5:33-34a, 37:

[33] Again you have heard that it was said to those of old, 'You shall not swear falsely, but shall perform your oaths to the Lord.' [34] But I say to you, do not swear at all... [37] But let your 'Yes' be 'Yes,' and your 'No,' 'No.' For whatever is more than these is from the evil one.

James 5:12:

> *But above all, my brethren, do not swear, either by heaven or by earth or with any other oath. But let your 'Yes' be 'Yes,' and your 'No,' 'No,' lest you fall into judgment.*

We understand many have already revoked curses due to these organizations, but our goal is to set our regions and families free. In the process, you might see a step you may have left out in your prayers. We could think we are divorced from these gods and may not. I say this because of the sin god allah and certain rights connected to other entities that may have been taken without a person's knowledge.

Our purpose is to recover ourselves and our region from the snare of the devil, who has taken many into captivity without their knowledge. At the conclusion, we will request a Cease-and-Desist order against the sin god allah to be issued by the Judge in our region, territory, and families.

2 Timothy 2:24:

> *And that they may come to their senses and escape the snare of the devil, having been taken captive by him to do his will.*

The following is a brief overview of each of these eight organizations and their required vows. We will then agree with a prayer of repentance over each one of those issues individually and renounce each of their required oaths and vows.

Who is allah?

He is the god over the Shriners, Masons, and Eastern Star Orders.

Shriner Involvement

If you have a family member who was a Shriner, you will want to read this next session closely. If you have supported them in any way, the false gods behind their activities consider that you have condoned what they do and are in support of them. They often participate in parades and community fundraising activities. They appeal to support hospitals for burn victims or disabled children...all good works, through fish fries and other activities.

The crescent moon and star are the emblem or symbol Shriners proudly wear. To wear the hat and jacket with emblems, one speaks vows and oaths. The hat, called a Fez, has a crescent and a star.

A Shriner is given a red fez with an Islamic sword and crescent jewel on the front of it. This sword emblem originates from the seventh century when Muslims, under the leadership of Muhammad (aka Mohammed), slaughtered all Christians and Jews who would not bow down to the pagan moon god allah. It is a symbol of subjugation.

The Shriners began innocently enough, except for their link to and allegiance to the pagan moon god (note the crescent emblem) allah. Candidates for induction into the Shriners are greeted by a High Priest, who says:

> *By the existence of allah and the creed of Mohammed; by the legendary sanctity of our Tabernacle at Mecca, we greet you.*

The inductees then swear on the Bible and the Koran in the name of Mohammed and invoke Freemasonry's usual gruesome penalties upon themselves:

> *I do hereby, upon this Bible, and on the mysterious legend of the Koran and its dedication to the Mohammedan faith, promise, swear, and vow...that I will never reveal any secret part or portion whatsoever of the ceremonies...and now upon this sacred book, by the sincerity of a Moslem's oath, I here registered this irrevocable vow...in willful violation whereof may I incur the fearful penalty of having my eyeballs pierced to the center with a three-edged blade, my feet flayed, and I be forced to walk the hot sands upon the sterile shores of the Red Sea until the flaming sun shall strike me with livid plague, and may Allah, the god of Arab, Moslem and Mohammedan, the god of our fathers, support me to the entire fulfillment of the same. Amen. Amen. Amen.*

Muslim is the preferred term for "follower of Islam," although Moslem is also widely used.[12]

With this oath, in their ignorance, people who consider themselves Christians swear on the Koran and declare Allah to be "the god of our fathers." From the perspective of Christianity and Islam alike, Shriners take the name of God in vain and mock both faiths.

Irrevocable Vow

Interestingly, they have to say amen three times to establish what they are agreeing to. We see an example of this in the Bible with the example of Peter. In Mark 14:66-72, he swears three times that he does not know Jesus. This pattern indicates he needed to say something three times to emphasize that he was rejecting Christ, which he did. We see that doing so even removed him from being considered a disciple by Christ himself. To be reinstated, Jesus asked Peter to repeat three times that he loved him to revoke his previous denial and reinstate him in his earlier position.

> ...go, tell His disciples—and Peter—that He is going before you into Galilee; there you will see Him, as He said to you. (Mark 16:7)

---

[12] https://www.quora.com/What-is-the-difference-between-the-Words-Moslem-and-Muslim

We see that a person can be restored to Jesus and oaths forgiven, but something needs to be done about it. The vow does not just remove itself; the curse will not voluntarily leave either. As we pray this prayer, you may see and repent for things that were not in the description of their vows but are based on some original activity of this organization.

Prayer of Repentance

We come humbly before you into the Courtroom of Heaven. We understand there are many people in our region and our family bloodlines who this particular type of sin has corrupted.

We stand in the gap and repent on behalf of the sin committed by any people within the regions and territories represented and any member of our generational bloodlines who has recited and agreed with these oaths and vows made to allah through the organization of the Shriners.

We renounce the oaths and actions performed in any of these rites. We renounce the curses and their penalties involved in the Ancient Arabic Order of the Nobles of the Mystic Shrine. We ask forgiveness for this sin of worship of allah in this region and ask for the blood of Jesus to cover over and cut off from any curses connected with this, our region, each of us, and all members of our generational bloodlines who are still alive and yet to come.

We renounce and ask that this curse be broken and that every associated demon and principality working through these curses leave now.

[Expel through blowing or coughing]

We say, "The Lord rebuke you. You no longer have any legal right to stay!"

We petition you, Lord, to restore what the locust has stolen from us, our families, and this region.

We ask you to release the blessings and the healings you have for us.

We ask that you remove this god and his influence from our region and territory.

We ask that divine revelation will come to those ensnared by this god.

We entreat you, Jesus, the light of the world: Speak to them in dreams and visions. Reveal your truth. We say they will see the truth, embrace it, and walk in it. Amen.

. . .

Masonic Lodge Members

1st Degree

These oaths are found in several Masonic publications, including *Duncan's Masonic Ritual and*

Moniter and *Look to the East*, a ritual of the first three degrees of Masonry.

The oath taken by the candidate for Entered Apprentice is:

> *I, _____, of my own free will and accord, in the presence of Almighty God, and this Worshipful Lodge erected to him and dedicated to the Holy Saint John, do hereby and hereon (Master presses his gavel on candidate's knuckles) most hail, forever conceal, never reveal any of the secret arts, parts or points of the hidden mysteries of Masonry which may have been heretofore, or shall be, at this time, or at any future period, communicated to me as such, to any person or persons whomsoever, except it be a true and lawful brother Mason, or within the body of a just and lawfully constituted Lodge of Masons. All this I most solemnly and sincerely promise and swear, with a firm and steadfast resolution to keep and perform the same, without the least equivocation, mental reservation or secret evasion whatsoever; binding myself under no less penalty than that of having my throat cut from ear to ear, my tongue torn out by its roots, and buried in the sands of the sea, at low-water mark, where the tide ebbs and flows twice in twenty-four hours, should I, in the least, knowingly or wittingly violate or transgress this my Entered Apprentice*

> obligation. So, help me God, and keep me steadfast (Look to The East, pp. 30, 31).
>
> I promise and swear that I will not cheat, wrong, or defraud a Lodge of Fellow Crafts, brother of this degree, knowingly or wittingly.
>
> All this I most solemnly and sincerely promise and swear, with a firm and steadfast resolution to keep and perform the same, without the least equivocation, mental reservation or self-evasion whatsoever; binding myself under no less penalty than that of having my left breast torn open, my heart plucked from thence, and given to the beasts of the field and the birds of the air as a prey, should I, in the least, knowingly or wittingly, violate or transgress this my Fellow Craft obligation. So, help me God and keep me steadfast (Ibid., p. 96).

Some lodge members might say they do not take these oaths seriously and do not feel bound by them. Yet, Jesus says we should not engage in false, profane, or frivolous swearing. (Matthew 5:33-37)

If Masons take these oaths seriously, they stand condemned for taking such profane oaths. If they do not take them seriously and do not feel bound by them, they still stand condemned for such frivolous swearing and using the name of God in such a manner. After making each oath, the candidate is asked to kiss the Bible (which is a DNA exchange). This might be the reason some are fooled into thinking this is approved by God in some twisted way, especially if they are a new Christian. The Lord warns us about making vows.

James 5:12:

But above all, my brethren, do not swear, either by heaven or by earth or with any other oath. But let your 'Yes' be 'Yes,' and your 'No,' 'No,' lest you fall into judgment.

Repentance Prayer & Petition

We repent for sin committed by anyone from our generational bloodlines and on behalf of any of those in our region and territory who have recited and enacted the vows and oaths required to join the Masonic Lodge.

We ask forgiveness for this sin, which pledges allegiance to the foreign god of allah. We ask for Jesus's blood to cover these sins and wash the people clean. We ask You to cut off from us the curses and their consequences as a result of these vows and oaths.

We renounce the oaths taken and the curses involved in the First or Entered Apprentice degree, especially their effects on the throat and tongue.

We renounce the hoodwink, the blindfold, and its effects on emotions and eyes, including all confusion, fear of the dark, fear of the light, and fear of sudden noises.

We renounce the secret word Boaz and all it means.

We renounce the mixing and mingling of truth and error and the blasphemy of this degree of Masonry.

We renounce the noose around the neck, the fear of choking, and also every spirit causing asthma, hay fever, emphysema, or any other breathing difficulty.

We renounce the compass point, sword or spear held against the breast, the fear of death by stabbing pain, and the fear of heart attack from this degree.

In the name and through the blood of Jesus Christ, we now pray for healing of the throat, vocal cords, nasal passages, sinus, bronchial tubes, and lungs, and for healing of the speech area and the release of the Word of God to me and through me and my family and throughout our region and territory which will bring revival and the Glory of God.

We renounce and command this curse and any accompanying demons and principalities to leave now. You no longer have any legal right to stay.

I petition You, Lord, to remove the veils from the eyes of the understanding of those snared and netted by the enemy and still active in this organization. Show them the truth.

We ask for a freedom of information act to be released even through the media about the truth of these organizations and other things that this god, allah, has hidden.

We pray for the seed of Abraham, who live in our area, to be awakened to the truth through any means You want to employ as the one true and living God.

We thank You for the salvation and revival that will occur as You grant us our divorce from this god.

We ask You to restore what the locust has stolen from me and to the rest of my family the blessings and the healings that You have for us. Amen.

. . .

2nd Degree

The Fellow Craft (Second Degree) candidate makes a vow similar to that taken by the Entered Apprentice.

Repentance Prayer & Petition

We stand in the gap and repent on behalf of any member of our generational bloodlines and any who live in our region and territory or who will reside here in the future and have recited and agreed with these oaths and vows.

We ask forgiveness for this sin of the worship of the foreign god allah and ask for the blood of Jesus to cover over and cut us and anyone else involved from all curses connected with this.

We renounce the oaths taken and the curses involved in the second or Fellow Craft degree of Masonry, especially the curses on the heart and chest. We renounce the secret words JACHIN and SHIBBOLETH and all that these mean.

We cut off emotional hardness, apathy, indifference, unbelief, and deep anger from this region and my family and me.

In the name and through the blood of Jesus Christ, we pray for healing of the chest/lung/heart area and the healing of emotions and ask to be made sensitive to Holy Spirit of God.

As we renounce these oaths and vows and command this curse and its demons to leave, they must go. They no longer have a legal right to stay.

We petition You, Lord, to restore what the locust has eaten from the people of our region, me personally and the rest of my family, the blessings and the healings that You have for us. Amen.

. . .

3rd Degree

The oath taken by Master Masons (Third degree) includes many of the same affirmations as the first two.

Repentance Prayer & Petition

We stand in the gap and repent for any member of our generational bloodlines who recited and agreed with these oaths and vows.

We ask forgiveness for this sin of the worship of a foreign god and ask for the blood of Jesus to cover over and cut us and the members of our generational bloodlines who are still alive and yet to come off from any curses connected with this.

We stand in the gap and repent for those in this region and territory who have taken part in any of these oaths and vows.

We ask forgiveness on their behalf and ask You to move any case the enemy has against them to the Throne of Grace and Mercy, where You will remove the veils from the eyes of their understanding, and they will see the truth and embrace the truth and walk in the truth.

We renounce the oaths taken and the curses involved in the third or Master Mason degree, especially the curses on the stomach and womb area. I renounce all secret words and all that they mean.

We renounce the Spirit of Death from the blows to the head enacted as ritual murder, the fear of death, false martyrdom, fear of violent gang attack, assault or rape, and the helplessness of this degree.

We renounce falling into the coffin or stretcher involved in the ritual of murder.

We renounce the false resurrection of this degree because only Jesus Christ is the Resurrection and the Life!

We also renounce the blasphemous kissing of the Bible on a witchcraft oath.

We renounce and cut off all spirits of death, witchcraft, and deception.

In the name and through the blood of Jesus Christ, we pray for the healing of the stomach, gall bladder, womb, liver, and any other organs of our body affected by Freemasonry. We ask for a release of compassion and understanding for our family and us.

. . .

31st Degree

Repentance Prayer & Petition

We stand in the gap and repent on behalf of any member of our generational bloodline and any who live in our region and territory or who will reside here in the future and have recited and agreed with these oaths and vows.

We ask forgiveness for this sin of worship of the foreign god allah and ask for the blood of Jesus to cover over and cut us and anyone else involved from all curses connected with this off from the consequences and heal us and others involved.

We renounce the oaths taken and the curses involved in the thirty-first degree of Masonry, the Grand Inspector Inquisitor Commander.

We renounce all the gods and goddesses of Egypt, which are honored in this degree, including Anubis with the ram's head, Osiris the Sun god, Isis the sister and wife of

Osiris, and the moon goddess. We renounce the Soul of Cheres, the false symbol of immortality, the Chamber of the Dead, and the false teaching of reincarnation.

We ask that You move everyone who has had a part in this to the Throne of Grace and Mercy and remove the veils off of their understanding so that they will embrace the truth and walk in truth.

. . .

32nd Degree

Repentance Prayer & Petition

We stand in the gap and repent on behalf of any member of our generational bloodline and any living in this region and territory or residing here in the future who have recited and agreed with these oaths and vows.

We ask forgiveness for this sin of the worship of the foreign god allah and ask for the blood of Jesus to cover over and cut us and anyone else involved from all curses connected with this.

We renounce the oaths taken and the curses involved in the thirty-second degree of Freemasonry, the Sublime Prince of the Royal Secret.

We renounce masonry's false trinitarian deity AUM and its parts, Brahma the creator, Vishnu the preserver and Shiva the destroyer.

We renounce the deity of AHURA-MAZDA, the claimed spirit or source of all light, and the worship with fire, which is an abomination to God, and also the drinking from a human skull in many Rites.

...

33rd Degree

Repentance Prayer & Petition

We stand in the gap on behalf of anyone in our generational bloodlines and anyone in our region and territory who has spoken and rehearsed these vows and oaths, and we ask forgiveness for this sin.

In the name of Jesus Christ, we renounce the oaths taken and the curses involved in the supreme thirty-third degree of Freemasonry, the Grand Sovereign Inspector General.

We renounce the secret passwords.

We renounce all the obligations of every Masonic degree and all penalties invoked. We renounce and utterly forsake The Great Architect of the Universe, who is revealed in this degree as Lucifer, and his false claim to be the universal fatherhood of God.

We renounce the cable-tow around the neck.

We renounce the death wish that the wine drunk from a human skull should turn to poison and the skeleton whose cold arms are invited if the oath of this degree is violated.

We renounce the three infamous assassins of their grand master, law, property, and religion, and the greed and witchcraft involved in the attempt to manipulate and control the rest of mankind.

In the name of God, the Father, Jesus Christ the Son, and Holy Spirit, we renounce and break the curses involved in the idolatry, blasphemy, secrecy, and deception of Freemasonry at every level, and we appropriate the Blood of Jesus Christ to cleanse all the consequences of these from our life.

We now revoke all previous consent given by us, or any of our ancestors, or anyone in our region or territory to be deceived. We renounce the All-Seeing Third Eye of Freemasonry or Horus in the forehead and its pagan and occult symbolism.

We renounce all false communions taken, all mockery of the redemptive work of Jesus Christ on the cross of Calvary, all unbelief, confusion, and depression, and all worship of Lucifer as God.

We renounce and forsake the lie of Freemasonry that man is not sinful but merely imperfect and can redeem himself through good works.

We rejoice that the Bible states that we cannot do a single thing to earn our salvation but that we can only be saved by grace through faith in Jesus Christ and what He accomplished on the Cross of Calvary.

We renounce all fear of insanity, anguish, death wishes, suicide, and death in the name of Jesus Christ.

Jesus Christ conquered death, and He alone holds the keys of death and hell, and I rejoice that He has my life in His hands now. He came to give me life abundantly and eternally, and I believe in His promises.

We renounce all anger, hatred, murderous thoughts, revenge, retaliation, spiritual apathy, false religion, all unbelief, especially unbelief in the Holy Bible as God's Word, and all compromise of God's Word.

We renounce all spiritual searching into false religions and all striving to please God. We rest in the knowledge that we have found our Lord and Savior, Jesus Christ, and that He has found us.

We will burn all objects in our possession that connect us with all lodges and or cultic organizations, including Freemasonry, witchcraft, and Mormonism and all regalia, aprons, books of rituals, rings, and other jewelry. We renounce the effects that these or other objects of Freemasonry, such as the compass, the square, the noose, the blindfold, or the apron have had on me or my family, in Jesus' name.

A more complete court case regarding freedom from Freemasonry as well as freedom from Mithraism is available on our website:

RonHorner.com

———— ∞ ————

Resources from LifeSpring International Ministries

A visit to the **RonHorner.com** website will give a glimpse of the various branches of ministry we are involved in. We started providing coaching to people within the Courts of Heaven advocating for them and their situations. Our corporate name is LifeSpring International Ministries, Inc., a North Carolina registered nonprofit.

Personal Advocacy Sessions

Known as Personal Advocacy Sessions, these 90-minute sessions with our trained team of advocates have successfully worked with a myriad of situations. If you have an issue that you can't seem to get breakthrough about, schedule a session with our advocates.

LifeSpring Mentoring Group

Since starting this weekly class on Zoom in 2019, we have taught on the Courts of Heaven, protocols, engaging Heaven for revelation, working with angels and men and women in white linen, lingering human spirits, and more. It is a free class. Simply visit **ronhorner.com** to register for the link for the class.

Membership Program

We have several tiers of membership for those tracking with us. The Platinum level gains you access to our library of videos, blogs, and more. Again, visit the website.

LifeSpring School of Ministry

A trimester-based school to help you grow in your walk. Trimester 1 focuses on cleansing your generations. Trimester 2 focuses on Protocols of the Courts of Heaven, and Trimester 3 focuses on Advanced Protocols of the Courts of Heaven. Completion of Trimesters 1, 2, and 3 will qualify the student for consideration as a Junior or Senior Advocate able to conduct Personal Advocacy Sessions with our clients.

CourtsNet

CourtsNet is our video-based training program offering a wide variety of classes and courses. We have free courses as well as paid courses.

AfterCare

Not every situation is solved by the Courts of Heaven. Sometimes people need to learn simple things to navigate life. Our AfterCare program provides Biblical counseling, classes, and groups regularly.

Sandhills Ecclesia

In 2022, we began a Sunday Gathering known as Sandhills Ecclesia, which is the name we saw on the book in Heaven when we went to inquire. My wife, Adina, and I live in the North Carolina area known as the Sandhills region, hence the name. We meet weekly at 11:00 AM Eastern Time, and on the first Sunday of each month, we have an afternoon gathering to conduct legislative work in the Courts of Heaven as a group. All are welcome. Simply visit **sandhillsecclesia.com** and register for the link.

Heaven Down Business

Heaven Down Business is a worldwide coaching and consultancy business designed to assist entrepreneurs and business owners in implementing the Heaven Down™ Business Building paradigm into their business. For more information, visit **heavendownbusiness.com**.

Adina's Melodies/Heaven Down Music

Adina Horner, co-founder, is a gifted minstrel and has several albums of prophetic worship music available on several of the most popular music platforms. Visit **adinasmelodies.com**.

LifeSpring Publishing/Scroll Publishers

LifeSpring Publishing primarily publishes Dr. Ron's books, and Scroll Publishers is our imprint where we publish the books of others relating to engaging Heaven, living spirit forward, and the Heaven Down™ lifestyle.

YouTube Channel

Our most recent videos from the Mentoring Group are posted on YouTube®. Visit our YouTube® channel,

courtsofheavenwebinar on YouTube® for the latest videos.

RonHorner.com

Our website, **RonHorner.com,** has a myriad of resources, many of which are free, as well as numerous videos.

———— ∞ ————

Description

Embracing Crowns for Governmental Intercession is a powerful call to believers who sense a divine pull to pray beyond personal needs and into realms of influence, authority, and heavenly mandates. This book unveils the truth that you were born not just to intercede but to govern in prayer—wearing crowns of spiritual authority and aligning with God's Kingdom purposes on Earth.

This guide empowers you to move from passive prayer to strategic intercession that shapes nations, unlocks destinies, and dismantles darkness. Whether you're new to intercession or a seasoned warrior, you'll discover how to embrace your God-given crowns, step into your spiritual identity, and partner with Heaven to bring transformation to governments, systems, and societies.

It's time to rise—not just as a voice—but as a vessel of royal authority. It's time to embrace your crown and take your place. You were born crowned. Now, it's time to understand what has been poured into yours—and why it changes everything.

——— ∞ ———

About the Author

Dr. Ron Horner is an apostolic teacher specializing in the Courts of Heaven. He has written nearly forty books on the Courts of Heaven, engaging Heaven, working with angels, living from revelation, and most recently, about Crowns of Authority.

He currently trains people in engaging the Courts of Heaven in a weekly online teaching session. You can register to participate and discover more about the Courts of Heaven prayer paradigm on his various websites, classes, products, and services found here:

www.ronhorner.com

Other Books by Dr. Ron M. Horner

Building Your Business from Heaven Down

Building Your Business from Heaven Down 2.0

Building Your Business with the Blueprint of Heaven

Commissioning Angels – Volume 1

Cooperating with The Glory

Courts of Heaven Process Charts

Dealing with Trusts & Consequential Liens

Embracing Your Crown of Authority

Embracing Crowns for Governmental Intercession

Embracing Crowns for Your Business

Embracing Crowns for Your Family

Engaging Angels in the Realms of Heaven

Engaging Heaven for Revelation – Volume 1

Engaging Heaven for Revelation – Volume 2

Engaging Heaven for Trade

Engaging the Courts for Ownership & Order

Engaging the Courts for Your City (*Paperback, Leader's Guide & Workbook*)

Engaging the Courts of Healing & the Healing Garden

Engaging the Courts of Heaven

Engaging the Help Desk of the Courts of Heaven

Four Keys to Dismantling Accusations

Freedom from Mithraism

Kingdom Dynamics – Volume 1

Kingdom Dynamics – Volume 2

Let's Get it Right!

Lingering Human Spirits

Lingering Human Spirits – Volume 2

Living Spirit Forward

Maximizing Your Crown of Authority

Next Dimension Access to the Court of Supplications

Overcoming the False Verdicts of Freemasonry

Overcoming Verdicts from the Courts of Hell

Releasing Bonds from the Courts of Heaven

The Courts of Heaven: An Introduction
(formerly *Engaging the Mercy Court of Heaven*)

Unlocking Spiritual Seeing

Working with Your Realms and Your Realm Angels

SPANISH

Cómo Anular los Falsos Veredictos de la Masonería

Cómo Proceder en la Corte Celestial de Misericordia

Cómo Proceder en las Cortes para su Ciudad

Cómo Trabajar con Angeles en los Ambitos del Cielo

Cooperando con La Gloria de Dios

Las Cuatro Llaves para Anular las Acusaciones

Liberando Bonos en las Cortes Celestiales

Liberando Su Visión Espiritual

Sea Libre del Mitraísmo

Tablas de Proceso de la Cortes del Cielo

———— ∞ ————

www.ingramcontent.com/pod-product-compliance
Lightning Source LLC
Chambersburg PA
CBHW021135230426
43667CB00005B/120